Angela Lansbury's

POSITIVE
MOVES

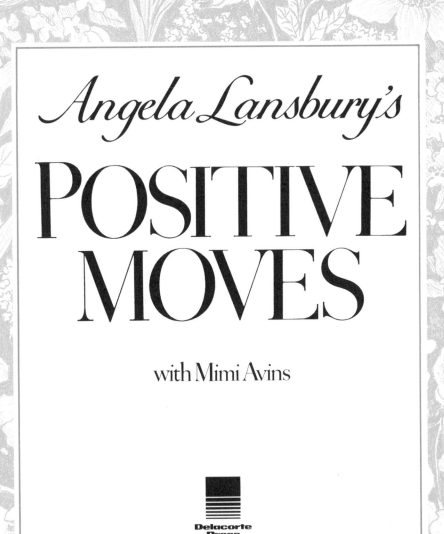

Angela Lansbury's

POSITIVE MOVES

with Mimi Avins

Delacorte Press

The advice and exercises in this book are intended to be used only in conjunction with the advice of your own personal physician. Because of the differences in physical conditioning from individual to individual, your doctor should make sure that these exercises are safe for you. Consult your physician before performing this or any other exercise program.

Photo Credits: page 11, The *Silver Screen* Archives; pages 12–13, *National Velvet—Movie Star News; The Harvey Girls*—MGM Studios; page 20, *Dear World*—UPI Photo; *Gypsy*—Martha Sloope; page 107, Tony Esparza; page 144, A/P Wide World Photos; pages 28, 32, 39, 45, 65, 69, 73, 77, 88, 98, 115, 119, 124, 134, 136, 156, Philip Saltonstall.

Published by
Delacorte Press
Bantam Doubleday Dell Publishing Group, Inc.
666 Fifth Avenue
New York, New York 10103

Library of Congress Cataloging in Publication Data

Lansbury, Angela
[Positive moves]
Angela Lansbury's positive moves : my personal plan for fitness and well-being / with Mimi Avins.
p. cm.
ISBN 0-385-30223-1
1. Physical fitness. 2. Physical fitness—Psychological aspects.
3. Health. 4. Beauty, Personal. I. Avins, Mimi. II. Title.
III. Title: Positive moves.
GV481.L35 1990
613.7—dc20 90-3291 CIP

Manufactured in the United States of America

Published simultaneously in Canada

November 1990

10 9 8 7 6 5 4 3 2 1
RRH

To Moyna,
my inspiration then and always.

Acknowledgments

There are many dear people who have helped me write this book:

My thanks and appreciation to Carole Baron and Isabel Geffner, who suggested I attempt this book in the first place.

To Mimi Avins, my friend and collaborator, who compiled and edited the many conversations we had and helped me shape the material into a logical progression of thoughts and conclusions on the subject of health and fitness.

To Judy Gantz, who encouraged and helped me to seek out and develop the best possible exercise regimen to enhance and maintain grace and suppleness.

To Betsy Knapp, of Wood Knapp, Inc., who went along with my dream to create my video *Positive Moves* on which this book is based.

To Dolores Childers, my dear friend and assistant, who never failed to tell me when my slip was showing.

To my son David, who launched the whole project and kept the lines of communication open between us girls.

To my husband, Peter, whose good taste and encouragement throughout made it all possible in the first place.

To all my beloved family, who took this book as seriously as I have. I hope that they will reap the benefits in the years to come.

And finally, to the many terrific nameless women of a certain age who wrote and asked me to tell them how I did it.

Contents

1

Living with a Positive Attitude

AN INTRODUCTION

Southern California, where I have lived for the past six years, is known for its clear skies and brilliant sunlight. But every now and then a thick fog, what we used to call a real "pea souper" in London, will roll in from the Pacific. My house, perched up on a wooded hillside, becomes enveloped by mist. At such times, I love to light a fire and settle down in a big, comfy chair to read a stack of letters.

They come from all over the country, from young mothers and middle-aged schoolteachers, from women who are everything from business executives to artists. The letters are all different, and yet, certain themes recur in my mail. "How do you manage to have so much energy?" "How do you continue to look so vital at your age?" (Good Lord—that makes me sound ninety-nine!) "How do you stay so trim?"

Some of these questions are directed to the marvelous fictional character that I portray, mystery writer Jessica Fletcher. To an extent, the public mentally blends us into one woman. While we have our differences, I actually do know something about some of the qualities for which Jessica is admired: her energy, her optimism and curiosity. And I realize that those qualities have become increasingly valued as more and more people live longer lives. Today, a woman in her sixties probably has twenty or twenty-five years ahead of her. Yet, as we mature as women, we become increasingly aware that it isn't as easy as it used to be to lead the vigorous, active lives that we enjoyed as youngsters.

I was throwing a ball with my grandson the other day. I threw it the way I normally do, and I felt a sudden stab of pain as I pulled a muscle. It reminded me that the years go by, and one must remember that the joints become stiff, the muscles might not all do what you expect them to. (It didn't stop me from tossing the ball again, of course.) Sharing activities with my grandchildren is one of the great joys of my life, but I know that as I advance in years, if I want to continue to be physically active, then preparing the body is essential.

I think it's never too late to take certain measures to maintain our mobility, muscular strength, and ability to move gracefully. Although I'm not a fitness expert or a dietician or a fanatic about any of this health business, I am vitally interested, as I'm sure you are, in finding ways to create a life-style that will allow me to continue to enjoy the things I did when I was younger.

As we grow older, I wonder whether much of our behavior alters because we feel differently and respond to real physical changes, or because we think we are expected to behave a certain way in order to "act our age." My mail tells me that people enjoy seeing me not behaving like a woman of my years. Week after week, Jessica Fletcher proves that "women of a certain age" don't have to take a backseat to the younger crowd. We women of a certain age can still accomplish things, continue to be adventurous and outgoing. We can still look attractive. We can look forward to a promising future, not merely settle for a sedentary old age. The message I get from people of many different ages is that we aren't looking for some sort of magical fountain of youth, but we do think it's worth the effort to find a realistic way to enjoy our later years.

It isn't surprising that most of us don't welcome the passing of time. None of us wants to face his or her own mortality. But growing older has some wonderful aspects. One does enjoy the benefits of wisdom and experience from the whole pile of life that's been lived. I know I can attribute some of my ability to work as hard as I do and still maintain my health and my zest for living to my professional education and experience. As an actress, I've had to pay attention to my body in a way that the average person normally doesn't. Of course, I have to stay at a certain weight for the camera (or I should!), but there is more I've acquired from my early dance training and my later experience in the theater that still serves me well today and can apply to everybody: a sense of my own posture and a body awareness that requires me to keep myself flexible and adaptable and conscious of how I move. I've found a series of gentle stretches and movements to be the most effective in helping me maintain my mobility and well-being, and I've included them all in the pages that follow.

To me, good health is more than just exercise and diet. It's really a point of view and a mental attitude you have about yourself. A strong, shapely body is of little use unless the person inside it greets each day with optimism. Each individual is different, and each of us is born with certain tendencies. Some of us are positive, forward-thinking souls, others somehow seem to enjoy depressing themselves with negative thoughts and attitudes. We are getting older, that's an incontrovertible fact, and it isn't smart or helpful to deny reality. But do we think of our later years as a time of inevitable infirmity, sickness, malfunction, and general inability to keep up and enjoy life? I've even seen people with chronic health problems overcome their disabilities by remaining hopeful about what they are able to do. Those people are still marvelous to be around. It's all attitude. They don't dwell on "poor little me." Their attitude is "Yes, I have some problems to deal with, but I won't let them color my relationships with my family and my friends. I'll handle what I have to, and still enjoy the good things in my life."

Being focused on the present has been a mental habit of mine since I was a teenager. For me, living in the present tense means starting right this minute, from here on, believing that I have the power to make my life as good as I want it to be. I'm careful not to fall into the trap of saying, "If only . . . I had done this or that." I think many of us tend to play that game when we're looking for a way to justify our failures. I would rather look forward than look for excuses in the past, because most of the time hindsight really isn't helpful. After all, the present is what we're involved in, in life, the only thing we can really do anything about. How are we going to deal with this next hour, this next day? Instead of worrying about an ankle that I strained last winter, I'm interested in what I'm going to do right now to be healthy and to do the best for myself.

I don't often take conventional, tried-and-true routes to achieving things. I have arrived where I am in my career and in my life by following a rather singular path. Whether the task at hand was singing, dancing, exercising, or riding a bicycle, I've always seen myself doing it, and found, when it came to the test, that I could do it. It isn't that I have a swelled head. But I do have an extraordinary belief in my ability to do what I set my mind to. What I do in the field of exercise comes out of the personal need that I feel at the moment. If I feel that my muscles aren't responding the way I need them to, I'll find a way to keep them as warmed up and limber as possible. I never set out to attain some abstract ideal of physical strength or fitness, to reach my maximum heart rate or an optimal percentage of body fat. I merely seek to achieve a realistic level of comfort and activity for my life.

The foundation of my attitude toward what is now called fitness was laid many years ago by my mother. When I was a very young child, she took me along with her when she joined a group of women who met once a week in Regents Park in London to practice movement and exercise. The group was called the League of Health and Beauty. There I was, an enthusiastic six-year-old, all dressed up in a little Greek tunic. We would practice walking on the grass with velvet doughnut-sorts of things on our heads. My mother would tell me how to lower my shoulders, walk straight, and center myself in order to walk properly. And we would do classical Greek dances, out in the fresh air. Isadora Duncan had shown the world a new, free style of dancing, and we were all eager to try those lovely, fluid movements.

All little girls love dressing up and dancing, moving lightly as they pretend to be sugarplum fairies. It suits their sense of fantasy. I was no exception. In the League of Health and Beauty I learned the dance movements that come rather naturally to all of us if we give ourselves the opportunity to experience moving freely. But more important, I learned an awareness of the body. By watching my young friends, my mother, and all the other women who gathered to celebrate health and beauty, I learned that females are graceful creatures, from the time they're tiny until they're in their nineties. My mother had the most beautiful face in the world, but she was quite pear-shaped, and had a terrible fight, all her life, with her weight. When we joined our friends in the League of Health and Beauty, she did the movements as well. It became obvious to me that the important thing was moving like a goddess, whether or not one actually was a sylph.

Dance was part of my entire upbringing. It seemed I was

*From swimming as a
youngster to my early days
in the League of Health
and Beauty (that's me in
the middle), I had an
awareness of my body . . .
and it seems I always had
a flair for the dramatic!*

always in some kind of dance class. It was even part of the curriculum at school. When I was twelve, I went to dancing school and learned ballet, tap dance, all different sorts of dancing. And acting was the family business. My father had passed away when I was nine, and my mother was an actress. I was trained and prepared to go into the theater. As part of my education, my mother instilled in me the idea that grace is the most important quality that an actress can have. It was understood that it was equally important to being a woman.

We left London and emigrated to New York in 1940, one month before the bombing of Britain began. Being uprooted in wartime was certainly not easy, but I think I was born with an optimistic spirit. I have always relished and enjoyed the challenges that life presented. Overcoming obstacles and working to better things always excited me. That, to me, was fun.

When we were settled in New York, I enrolled in drama school. My twin brothers, five years younger than I, had scholarships for a fine prep school, and my mother did what she could to find work. In drama school I plunged into a course of study that included training to move and walk wearing different costumes—wearing a bustle, for example. We studied fencing and movement (it would be called "stretching exercises" today). We learned how to use the skeletal structure of the body to illustrate a character—to move like an old person, an angry or sick or tired person. (I've often thought that because actresses learn so much about the body and how it appears when it's older, they know which postures to avoid as they themselves age.)

Mother went off to Canada on tour in a variety show for the Royal Canadian Air Force units training there. At the end of her tour, she went to Los Angeles, where a number of her friends from the British theater world were working. At the end of the summer I received a wire from her: "Suggest you put the boys in school, close up the apartment, and come out to Los Angeles."

I was sixteen years old. I realize now that I was more responsible than I would expect a sixteen-year-old to be. But the war bred that kind of self-reliance. I'd been taught how to iron my brothers' shirts and pack up their trunks. It had to be done, so I did it. I often think that those of us who grew up in the Depression have an ability to roll with the punches. Having endured some hard times, I know I appreciate what came my way much more than if it had just dropped into my lap. You take care of tomorrow more when you've come through a war. You learn to have respect—for relationships, for friends, for money. Everything becomes more acute. And perhaps I learned to respect my body and my abilities as well. I know I learned to just get on with it, to do what had to be done without the luxury of feeling helpless or sorry for myself. In fact, that would never have occurred to me.

The philosophy my mother passed on to me was that we must believe anything is possible, that we can utilize the energy we have to change circumstances, to achieve success in our field, and to have meaningful relationships with people. She encouraged me to be comfortable and happy within myself, and not to be driven by misgivings or demons of doubt.

With this wonderfully positive canon at my core, I characteristically drove myself to the limits of my energy. When I was younger, I didn't hesitate to burn the candle at both ends. It never occurred to me to curtail my social activities because I would need my strength to work the next morning. I figured I could do it all, and when you're young, you can and you do.

I was put under contract to MGM Studios when I was eighteen. There were no organized exercise classes for the young contract players then. It was up to us to be in shape, and I never thought much about it. We would rehearse as long as

It always pleased me when people said I resembled my mother, Moyna Macgill. Here we are together in 1944.

three weeks for a big musical number in a film like *The Harvey Girls,* and during those three weeks, I got in shape. Obviously, if you were Cyd Charisse, you were in ballet class every day, but my feeling was, when the situation presented itself, I would get myself together and rise to the occasion. I only went to dance classes when a role required me to. When you're young, your muscles are loose, and you really can't hurt yourself by doing some high kicks now and then.

Although I worked in movies, television, and the theater during the 1950s, those years were mostly happy and exciting because we were settling into our first homes and starting our family. I had married Peter Shaw, a gorgeous-looking young Englishman just out of the army, in 1949. Within a few years

Some of my favorite film roles were my earliest, like National Velvet *(1944) (Can you see Liz Taylor and Mickey Rooney in the background?),* The Picture of Dorian Gray *(1945), and* The Harvey Girls *(1946).*

we had a boy and a girl, and Peter's young son from his first marriage came to live with us. We were the Eisenhower-years dream pair, a typical fifties couple, with the obligatory station wagon and even a floppy old English sheepdog in the back.

I was so happy with my family then that if I worked, I considered it a lovely bonus. For example, I was in a movie called *Kind Lady* with Ethel Barrymore, and she became sick,

Peter and I were married in London in 1949. My mother and his father, Walter Pullen, stood up for us.

poor darling. We were laid off for three weeks, with pay. So that paid for a swimming pool. We called it the "Ethel Barrymore pool." The great Shakespearean actor Maurice Evans was in the movie too. I remember he came out to the house and helped us landscape the pool. He dug all the holes for the rosebushes.

We left that house a few years later and moved to Malibu, to a home that hung out over the ever-changing ocean. We lived a very outdoorsy kind of existence, a beach life. I was out in the sun all the time, in the garden or with the children, always in shorts or a bathing suit. I never questioned my figure in those days. I never felt fat, or worried about my legs. I always thought they were okay. You take a lot of things for granted when you're young. It doesn't occur to you that it isn't always going to be that way.

Of course, I was a working mother, but that label didn't carry with it all the baggage that it does now. Nevertheless, I suppose I felt very much the way young professional women do today. Part of me was dying to stay home with my children, and part of me enjoyed my work. There were times when the emotional stamina called for was almost more than I could muster, when I had to leave my children for months at a stretch. Although I hated being away from my children, in those days women weren't saddled with the mantle of guilt that they are now. For professional women, it was more accepted that they would hire people to help them look after the children. That's what I did. I hired a lovely Scottish woman who took care of what had to be done when I couldn't.

When I began doing long runs on Broadway in the 1960s, I usually managed to bring the children East with me. And I no longer took for granted being physically up to the demands of the work. For something like the musical *Mame*, I really had to train. Having just entered my forties, I was being asked to

Here's our young family in California in the late fifties.

perform a very active show eight times a week. More than anything, I felt the need to build stamina. For three weeks before rehearsals began, I worked out strenuously with a coach, building up wind. Beatrice Arthur and I did exercises at the ballet barre and on the floor, getting ourselves in shape and our figures in trim for those roles. It felt terrific.

I was spending a lot of time working in New York in those years, and while I loved its high-pitched excitement, I felt the need for a peaceful getaway place. So we bought a house in Ireland. I had spent time there as a child with my Irish grandmother, and my memories of Ireland were among my most treasured. The Georgian country home we fell in love with was a vicar's house built in 1825 in the middle of a twenty-acre piece of land, with a river that ran down the back of the property. It was the most idyllic setting you could imagine, in the temperate, damp south of Ireland. Our Malibu house was destroyed in a terrible fire in 1970, so for many years, our Irish house really was home base.

One of the things I found so attractive about my times in Ireland was that the environment required me to be very physical in dealing with everyday life. I would routinely take my bike into the little village nearby, or ride five miles to the larger town. Every day I would bring in the firewood, and cook everything from scratch under comparatively primitive conditions. We had a half-acre walled garden where we grew all our own vegetables, and we'd often trek down to "our river" to catch fish for dinner.

Living there was like going back in time. I started being aware of aspects of housekeeping that I hadn't ever addressed myself to—using real linens, for example, not the synthetics we all take for granted now. I remember being aware of all my senses, hearing the crunch of feet on the gravel driveway when guests would arrive for dinner, their way lit only by the stars. Or feeling the scratch of the woolen sweaters we always bundled ourselves in because the house wasn't very well heated. Being close to the elements and dealing with life on a very basic level fed me in every possible way. By returning to values I had learned in Ireland as a child, I got in touch with what the important things are to me—feeling useful and productive and at one with nature, with my family close around me. Ever since, wherever I am, I'm always trying to reduce my life to the most simple elements, looking to create those feelings of well-being, of peace and fulfillment, that I felt in Ireland.

Strengthened in every way by my time in Ireland, I wasn't about to let my health or state of mind suffer from overwork,

I have treasured memories from the days we lived in the Ireland house.

too much stress, or just not taking care of myself during the periods when I went back to work on Broadway. If I was prepared to carry a demanding show, like *Gypsy* or *Mame* or *Sweeney Todd*, I wouldn't think of shortchanging the management. As a star, I always wanted to give full measure. In order to do that, I knew that I had to follow certain guidelines.

I had to get to bed at a decent hour. I had to give up leisure time and personal pursuits and make the performance my absolute first priority. Laurence Olivier used to say that an actor needs the stamina of an athlete, and it's true. Projecting the voice out to the far reaches of a theater's audience, maintaining the physical attitude needed to stay in character, and ensuring that it all looks quite effortless require enormous physical strength and a kind of concentration that makes tremendous demands on one's whole system.

While I was careful to take care of my health in all the obvious ways, from getting enough rest to not overindulging in food or alcohol to staying out of drafts, I know an intangible element did a lot for my stamina at that time too. That was simple happiness. The shows I did, and my work in them, were so well received that I had a sense of being surrounded by a golden glow of acceptance. That kind of resounding approval breeds self-confidence and more positive energy than I knew I possessed.

All my youth, the idea that the most important thing was doing a good job had been instilled in me by my mother. The experience of giving as much as was necessary for the roles I did on Broadway taught me that if I'm going to do my best, I must protect my health. I have come to realize that women of a certain age who lead busy lives have to marshal their forces if they want to have the energy they need. If you like your job, or you like the things you do in your life, you want to enhance the enjoyment by feeling good while you're doing them.

Although I had performed onstage and in the movies for many years, the first season of *Murder, She Wrote* was a new experience for me, in many ways. We followed a schedule that was customary for one-hour weekly television series, which meant I was working fifteen or sixteen hours a day, five days a week.

The work part of it was easy, but the hours were bloody awful. I couldn't leave the lot, and I felt like a prisoner, trapped in my trailer–dressing room for hours, day after day. Out of frustration, I started to overeat. I became quite sedentary and overweight. Carrying around fifteen extra pounds, I didn't feel well. I had headaches and stomachaches, even heart palpitations (a classic symptom of stress). It was ridiculous. Here we

My years on the Broadway stage were very gratifying—and my roles were incredibly diverse, as you can see in these moments from Dear World, Gypsy, *and* Sweeney Todd.

were, a big hit show, and I was sick, overtired, overweight, and thoroughly miserable.

The problem was that no one was paying attention to the fact that no woman had ever done what I was doing in television. And they had forgotten they were dealing with a woman who was a good deal older than most of the youngsters who were doing television. I was being forced into a mold, of having to perform on a schedule that a younger person could do fairly easily, but I could not.

I called the head of Universal Television and said, "Look. I'm terribly sorry. I cannot continue on this basis." They were sort of appalled to think that they were going to have to change a scheduling rule that had been sacrosanct since the dawn of television. All I wanted was to work no more than twelve hours at a stretch, and if that meant it would take us eight days to complete a show instead of seven, then that's how it had to be. When I pointed out the problem, they realized that they were right in conceding to my demands, and they were very generous and sweet about it.

I had to take a stand and say, "This doesn't work for me. Let's find a solution that does." In my definition, being healthy involves taking charge of your life and making sure that you have enough rest, that your stress isn't too great. Instead of just living with anger and the physical consequences I was having, I thought about how I could reasonably modify the situation. It's very important for me to understand what my limitations are and not be afraid to establish ground rules for myself and ask that people understand and respect them. It's one thing to pay attention to what vitamins I'm taking and how much I weigh. But what can be just as important is getting in touch with my needs, and figuring out how to get them met.

A friend of mine who isn't in the entertainment business found herself in an analogous situation recently. Her daughter developed the convenient habit of leaving her three young children with Grandma for the afternoon, several times a week. My friend loves her family dearly, but taking care of three toddlers for hours and hours was just too much for her. She was feeling overburdened, nervous, and overtired, but didn't want to refuse. Her husband finally pointed out to her that she would be completely unavailable for baby-sitting if she got sick, which was what overextending herself seemed to be leading to. When she calmly explained to her daughter that caring for the children so often was wearing her out, they agreed that only one child at a time would be left with Grandma, and for a shorter stay. Until my friend spoke up, her daughter said she had no idea that her mother had had any problem with the arrangement.

Even though I asked for and got more reasonable working hours several years ago, the schedule I follow now is still quite demanding. I'm usually up at half past five, and I allow myself an hour to get up and get out. I do most of my own makeup at home. I leave the house at six-fifteen or six-thirty to drive to the studio or a location. Once at work, I continue for a total of twelve hours, and no more. I really hold the line on that. Usually, I'm home from work by seven or seven-thirty. I have a light dinner, and then I have to study my script for the next day, or I'll read the next week's script.

I am naturally active, whether doing things with my grandchildren (have you ever tried to keep up with a five-year-old?) or gardening or working. My activities and my regular exercise program keep me at a base level of fitness that I feel is adequate for the demands of my life and work. If tomorrow a role came up in which I had to dance for five minutes, or I decided to do a musical special for television, I'd go into training, just as I always have. My life-style has given me an underlying confidence that I can whip myself into shape to meet the demands of my work. If I'm not being asked to do something that involves great physical effort, I don't bother keeping myself at a heroic level of performance.

I often say to myself, "Wow, you're having a good time. Will you still be the same when you're eighty?" And why wouldn't I be? Why not? I am continuously beginning. Everything I do is another step toward growing up, to attaining the optimum. I aspire to do interesting, fascinating, extraordinary things. The only thing that stops me, sometimes, is my inability physically to do the things I want to do. So it becomes necessary to honor the body, to treat it gently so it will be as ready as possible to do all the things I have in mind.

Sometimes I have marvelous dreams in which I'm a dancer and I'm doing tremendous leaps, flying across the stage as if I were weightless and borne by a gust of wind. Then I wake up and find that physically I can't do that. But because such dreams are highly symbolic, in many ways I can soar as I did in my dream. And my goal, as much as it's possible, is to marry the dream to reality.

Sticking to routines that I've evolved over the years helps me be at my best. I am a person who likes routine. When I'm working, I always get up at the same time. It's important to me to allow enough time to do the things that I need to do to start off on a good day. I eat the same things when I'm working, because that suits me. If I suddenly go off and eat a huge lunch, it slows me down in the afternoon. In the pages that follow, I'd like to share with you my routine for living, exercising, and eating healthfully. My hope is that you will find elements in it that will bring you the sense of well-being that we all strive for, at any age.

I remember when my daughter-in-law, Lee, was pregnant with our first grandchild, she conscientiously read a slew of the popular books out on becoming a parent. She remarked on how often the experts contradicted each other. "When the baby cries," she told me, "some say pick him up. Others say don't pick him up, let him cry. Others say pick him up, but only one time." She was a bit confused by all the advice, but not really baffled. "I suppose I'll read all the books, take in the information they offer, and then, when the time comes, I'll do what feels right," she said. She had the good sense to trust herself, which is undoubtedly one of the reasons I now have three delightful grandchildren (about whom I am completely objective!).

Whenever I've trusted my instincts about what's best for me, it's worked out well. So if you take my "message" to its logical conclusion, you won't follow my recommendations wholesale. I invite you to consider the philosophy and activities that have been beneficial to me, but always respect your individuality and your knowledge of yourself. Remember, you know better than anyone what works best for you.

2

Greeting the Dawn

18 STRETCHES TO START YOUR DAY

Well before the sun rises most mornings, the alarm clock in my bedroom sounds its unforgiving ring. I slap it into silence, and even before I get out of bed, I bring my knees up to my chest. My eyes aren't really open yet and my mind is still treading that murky ground between sleep and consciousness. But when I get those knees up and I feel the stretch in my lower back, it's as if I've turned the key and started my engine.

I have a little routine that helps me to swing into action. Once out of bed, the first thing I do is face the bathroom mirror and fill up my lungs with air. I hold it, then very slowly exhale. I'll take five or six of these deep breaths. It's the single most brain-clearing thing I can do.

Taking breath into the lungs helps me clear that ragbag that I call my mind. That is, in fact, a lyric by Stephen Sondheim from *Follies*. It's one of my favorite lines, because that's the way my mind feels in the morning—like a ragbag. It has so many thoughts jumbled around in it. To try to differentiate between the unimportant and the important, and to consider what the day has in store for me, I need to get oxygen to my brain.

By the time I've done a few minutes of deep breathing, I can see the garden that lies beyond my bathroom's French doors in the soft, first light of day. The roses seem to stretch up to receive the sun's warmth. While I'm taking in air, there's a palms-upward movement I do that's like reaching for the sun.

When I "greet the dawn" each morning, I know I'm beginning my day in the best way possible.

When my children first went to school, they were taught to sing a jingle about reaching for the stars while stretching their little arms up. I often remember that when I take in a deep breath and open my arms, reaching for the sun that's come up, as if to greet me.

I'll get up 15 minutes earlier than I have to just to have this time to breathe in the morning. It's a moment for myself that gives me a sense of taking charge. I'm giving myself the opportunity to remember those thoughts, unfinished dreams and ideas that present themselves in a rush when we first emerge from sleep.

After you've slept on a problem, you can often see it in a much clearer light. The solution has arrived while you were sleeping, and there it is in the morning. I believe that by taking a moment to breathe in the morning, you take the time to recognize your solutions, to understand that you now know how to proceed with a problem that seemed like a muddle before you, literally, slept on it.

Next, I get into the shower and get a lot of hot water on my neck and my shoulders. I wash my hair every morning. It's the most marvelous feeling in the world. I feel a bit guilty about the amount of water I'm using, but I kind of justify it by reminding myself that it's great exercise to get my hands up there and scrub. We can lose the strength in our upper arms so easily if we don't use them. If I feel like it, I'll do a few stretches in the shower, similar to some of the ones you'll see in the pages that follow. By stretching and expanding my body with unrestricted gestures, I'm physically opening up, making my body ready to receive what it must in the course of the day. Gradually, my mind becomes ready to receive as well, prepared to handle the challenges the day will present.

After my shower, I rub down with a hard towel, to get the circulation going. Then I take an aloe lotion, warm it in the palm of my hand, and slather it all over my body. I find it so much more pleasant to use a lotion that comes in a big, widemouthed jar than to struggle with squeezing one of those annoying tubes. I like to use lots of lotion, and it's much quicker and easier to just dip your hand into a big vat of the stuff. As I'm rubbing the lotion into my skin, I give myself a minimassage. I use smooth, rhythmic movements to increase the blood circulation, and I make sure I get all those nasty places, like the upper arms, where women tend to collect fat. I'll grab those soft areas that annoy me, like the inside of my thighs, and give them a good pinch. I do a kneading motion, rather like I do when I make bread, and really push with the fingers.

It makes me feel good just to slap myself around a bit. But there's more value to this little ritual, I think. You need to learn to know your body, and by doing my minimassage each day I am, in a very real sense, staying in touch with my body. I can't help but be aware of the shape I'm in. Once you've really examined your body, you have faced the moment of truth. Then you can decide if you want to do anything to improve the situation.

You can't be healthy if you let your body go to seed. I'm a big one for walking around the house with no clothes on. I'm very modest, so, of course, I do it privately. I don't answer the door in the altogether! It's strictly for my own sense of freedom. I sleep without a nightie. I feel it's important to let your skin really breathe. I think getting air to the body first thing in the morning is great, if it's not too cold. And you're never as aware of your posture as when you don't have clothes on.

While I'm massaging I might do a little self-assessing, but I'm not too tough on myself. I think self-acceptance is vital. There are certain things about our bodies we cannot alter, because we are all products of our genetic heritage. I also keep in mind that there are many good reasons to settle for certain changes that are part and parcel of maturity. Give yourself a break—there's something to like in every body.

At this Point, I take time to focus on the day ahead. While I'm soothing my body with lotion, I concentrate on calming my thoughts as I anticipate the next sixteen hours. This is a wonderful moment to crystallize in my mind's eye the perfect day.

Each day brings with it a different set of events that has to be dealt with. I think about each demand that will present itself in the coming day, and I visualize myself meeting it, easily and well. I remind myself that I am going to try to live each moment with a sense of peace, harmony, and calm.

I make a concerted effort to banish any destructive attitudes I might have been holding in. There's a trick I use. When I catch myself saying "I can't do this," or "that won't work," or "I'm not good at that," I quickly say to myself, "Cancel that. I'm going to expect the best." It's important not to allow those self-defeating thoughts to become wedged in your mind. The problem is that we too often accept our worst judgments about ourselves and build on them until they actually become part of our physical makeup. The power of suggestion can work negatively as well as positively, if we let it.

It's important to me to spend a few minutes each morning quietly focusing on the day ahead.

At the beginning of filming a new television show, I might be concerned about working with actors whom I haven't met before. I might be worried about having a particularly long speech to remember. If I'm having some concerns about that, I might wonder if I'll have enough time in the car to study it. So, I'll imagine that there will be enough time in the car and I will arrive at work knowing that speech. I'll imagine it will take care of itself, and the scene will go swimmingly, and everyone will respond well and it will turn out to be a good day's work. We can become so paralyzed by our anxieties. Instead, I find that when I visualize myself succeeding, then I will.

Whether you're going to the dentist or coping with family problems or dealing with a difficult business situation, if you can anticipate it in a positive way and see yourself accomplishing it successfully, it's very helpful. In the morning, see yourself getting the phone call, being hired for the job, passing the test, being sought out by a friend. See yourself in your mind's eye feeling great, not tired, able to cope, opening a new window, refreshing a friendship, reaching out, cooking an old recipe. If you're not going off to a job, you need even more character than someone who does. It takes greater discipline to do your job alone at home than in an office with other people. We're all the same. We all wake up wondering, "How am I going to get through this day?" I believe in taking hold of life and making it work for you.

This visualization trick has served me well in the theater. All my life, I've seen myself on the stage, doing a performance well, and then I forget about it. I don't keep harping on it. I paint the mental picture of myself as the character I'm to play, and then I let it go. When I played a rather wild character in *Sweeney Todd* on Broadway, people would say to me, "How could you conceive of Nellie Lovett?" Well, I could conceive of Nellie Lovett because I thought about her a great deal and I knew her. It was a feast of a role, and once I saw myself as Nellie, for me to turn around and turn myself into that character was not a problem.

The technique is quite similar when I'm imagining myself as a character who will have a great day. I take that moment in the morning, and in my mind's eye I imagine myself coming to the end of the day feeling that I had done the best I could under the circumstances. It's the dawn of a new day, and anything is possible.

Even after a good, hot shower and my self-massage, I still feel the need to stretch. It is just a simple fact of life that the older I get, the stiffer and tighter I feel in the morning when I get out of bed. Consistent stretching is the only thing that helps me maintain flexibility. I try never to allow my muscles to tighten up to the point where they lose their flexibility.

I've developed a series of stretches that I do every morning for about 15 minutes. I've found that after doing these movements often, always in the same order, they've become second nature. My body naturally goes into gear, as it were. If you've ever played the piano, you know how it feels when your fingers seem to remember a piece of music on their own. The body does have its own memory, so in time you can enjoy doing these exercises without thinking about them, just as I do. You can't expect to do every movement as easily as you'd like if you haven't been active for a while. But if you start gradually and stay with it, you'll be amazed at your progress.

Every movement that I make is to enhance my feeling of well-being and to give me a sense of freedom about my body. I want to relieve the sense of pressure that can develop, the feeling that there is a weight resting on my shoulders. I want to lighten my body so it doesn't become a prison in which I am the captive of my aches and pains.

What interests me about exercise is how it makes me feel, not that it's building a muscle or reducing my inner thighs. I haven't the patience, nor am I that self-involved, that I'm worried about reducing my inner thighs. In fact, there is no such thing as spot reducing. You can tone a particular area, but the way it really works is that when you eat less and move more, you lose fat everywhere on your body—eventually even those places that most annoy you.

I give the illusion of being strong, but that's sometimes just an illusion. Like everyone, I can't do many of the things I used to. I can't touch my head down to my knees while sitting on the floor. I used to be able to do that without even warming up. I could do it again, after working at it for a week, stretching and going for the burn and all that, but why should I? Any exercise that absolutely knocks the stuffing out of you can't be good. I want to be as mobile and limber as I need to be. Right now, that doesn't include being able to touch my head to my knees.

Some years ago I used to get together with a group of my tennis buddies to exercise. What we did was nothing like the aerobics you see today—it was more like calisthenics. Joining that group to exercise was an atypical thing for me to do, because I've always been one to do things on my own. I'm a bit shy, and when you're a public person, it's easy to feel self-conscious. In a group there's always someone who does it better than anybody else, or who has better-looking muscles. It can be rather daunting.

By exercising by myself, the only discipline I have to answer to is my own. It isn't true for everyone, but I seem to function best when I'm the one cracking the whip. As a child, I couldn't bear to be told what to do. So I've always found it rather intimidating to have a trainer or a coach. For me, there's a great freedom in doing it myself.

I wear a loose-fitting cotton jumpsuit when I exercise, and I'm usually barefoot. Any comfortable outfit you can move well in will do. And I don't put anything on my skin when I exercise. When you perspire, impurities rise to the surface of the skin, and it's best to leave the skin as open as possible.

If you aren't comfortable standing, you can do these stretches while you're sitting in a chair. While I usually do them in the morning, you can take a moment to do them while you're sitting in your office, or even if you're stuck in an airplane seat for hours and hours. I think you'll find they help you relax no matter when or where you do them.

You shouldn't be in a hurry when doing these stretches. I often find that listening to soft music with a slow, regular beat helps me time my movements. Remember the piano theme that was used in the movie *Terms of Endearment*? That seems to set the right pace for me for these stretches, and it's one of those melodies I don't get tired of hearing over and over. I'm sure you have your own favorites. A steady 4/4 beat is the easiest to move along with.

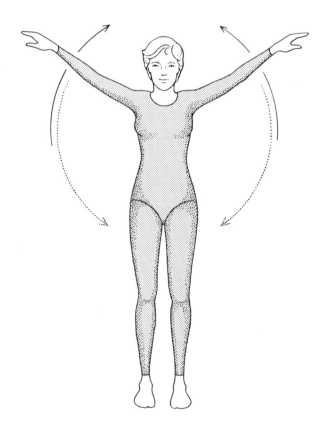

The first stretch I do in the morning uses the arms.

This deep breathing loosens the upper body and gets oxygen to the brain. In general, you should inhale as you initiate a movement, and exhale as you release. After you have done the exercises in this and the next chapter a few times, you'll find yourself breathing this way without even thinking about it.

Stand, with your legs comfortably apart and your knees relaxed, your arms at your sides. Breathing in, bring both arms up above your head. Then bring the arms back down, breathing out as you do. As you bring the arms up again, reach high and really take the air in. Then, slowly let your breath out as your arms come down. Be sure to take this slowly and gently. Hold your tummy in so your back doesn't arch. REPEAT FOUR TIMES.

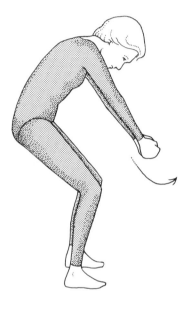

With your legs apart, your knees bent, and your arms in front of you, drop your head forward. Clasp your hands together and make a digging motion with them. Then let them hang to your knees. Your lower back should feel relaxed. Now gently pull in your stomach and round your back. Then, straighten up, letting your arms move up the length of your body till they're stretched up overhead. Slowly come back to your original position, keeping your hands clasped together. Drop down again. Your elbows can bend as your arms follow your body down. Tighten the stomach. Round the back. Then come up again, and back to your starting position. This movement is like a slow, graceful bow that stretches your back and shoulders. REPEAT FOUR TIMES.

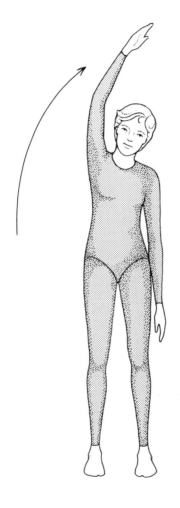

This movement helps keep your back flexible, and your carriage upright. You should feel a nice, long stretch through your waist as you do it. While I'm stretching, I think about the feeling of relief stretching gives me, especially when my body is feeling tight and cramped from inactivity.

Reaching your arm above your head, bend to the side, and let your hips move with you. Stretch your arm as far as you comfortably can, without bouncing, feeling the stretch in your waist. Make sure you draw in your stomach so you don't arch your back. ALTERNATE ARMS, REPEATING FOUR TIMES TO EACH SIDE.

The neck and shoulders carry so much tension, it's very important to warm up that area before doing more stretches.

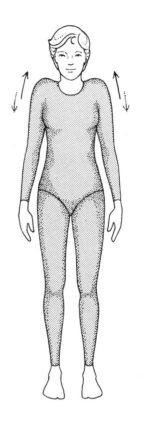

Inhale, lifting up both shoulders, and hold for a moment. Then release, exhaling and letting your shoulders drop with gravity. As you lift and drop the shoulders, your head doesn't really move. RE-PEAT THIS FIVE OR SIX TIMES, feeling more loose and free as you do it.

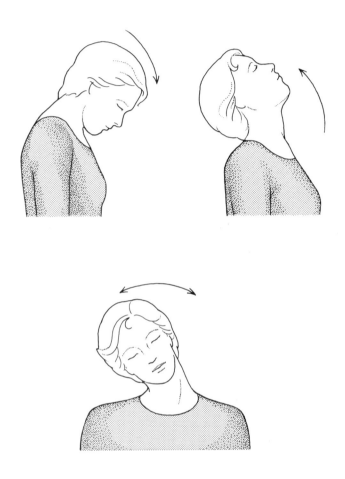

Think of this movement as reaching with the head, stretching up and out to loosen up those creaky neck muscles.

Try to move easily, and don't worry about getting it right. There's no wrong way to do these movements. Just feel free and loose and easy and light and, hopefully, graceful.

First, look down, tilting the head forward and stretching the back of the neck. Then, look up, reaching with the chin. Be careful not to tilt your head back too far when you're looking up. Tilt your head to the right, as if you were touching your ear to your shoulder, then tilt to the left, feeling the muscles at the sides of the neck stretching. REPEAT FRONT, BACK, SIDE, OTHER SIDE, FOUR TIMES.

These circular movements help release the shoulder and neck area. So often, I catch myself with my shoulders hunched if I don't watch it.

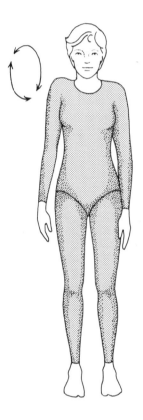

Gently move your shoulder in a circular motion, first from front to back, then circle it the other way. Keep the head and neck relaxed, and the head centered, not leaning to either side. **REPEAT FOUR TIMES WITH YOUR RIGHT SHOULDER, FOUR WITH THE LEFT, THEN FOUR TIMES EACH SIDE IN THE REVERSE DIRECTION.**

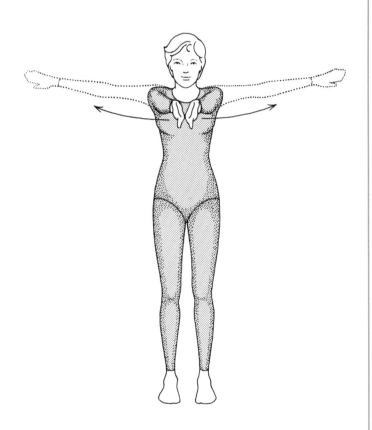

To open up the shoulders and the neck, I like to do a motion that is just like the breaststroke we do when we're swimming. I call these next two stretches on-land swimming.

Reach both arms straight out in front of you, with the thumbs touching. Then separate them, pushing all the way out to the side. Bring your hands together again at your chest, and push them out in front, repeating the motion. REPEAT SEVEN OR EIGHT TIMES.

When I do "on-land swimming" I feel so energized.

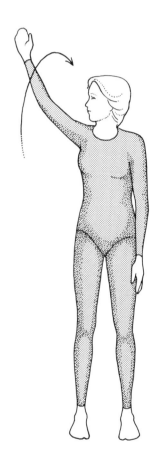

At first, you might feel literally like a fish out of water doing the breaststroke and the backstroke, but I think you'll like the feeling of opening up your arms, chest, spine, and waist.

Reach one arm back as you do when you're doing the backstroke, and let your head turn and follow your arm. It's okay to let your hips turn a little. Then, repeat the reach with the other arm. REPEAT SIX TIMES WITH EACH ARM.

For this stretch, I use a good-sized bath towel, roll it lengthwise, and get a good grip on the ends.

This helps correct rounded shoulders. As you stretch, stand as tall as you can. If you can't keep your arms up through four repetitions at first, don't worry. By doing this movement, in time you'll gain more strength in your arms. After a while, you should be able to keep them up longer without feeling tired. It's wonderful to build the strength in your arms. You want to be able to stretch to reach things, to be able to set your hair if you always have.

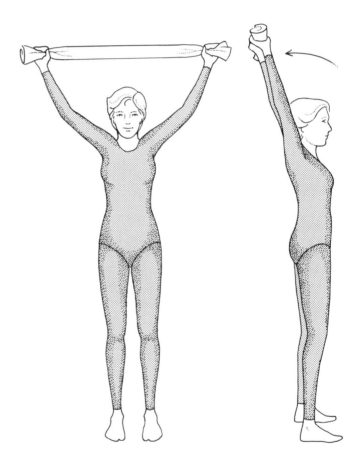

With both arms up, stretch the towel gently behind your head. Slowly pull the towel back, keeping your elbows straight, pulling gently back, only as far as you can. Bring the towel back over your head. REPEAT FOUR TIMES.

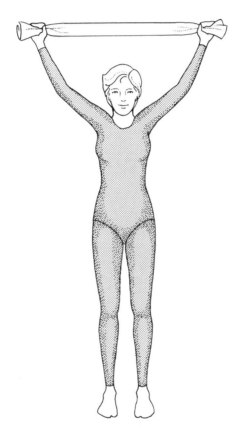

When we talk on the telephone or drive in stop-and-go traffic, we hold a lot of tension in the neck. This stretch loosens up those poor neck muscles we abuse all day.

While holding the towel overhead and your arms straight, turn your head to the side as far as it will go, first to one side, then the other. Try to keep your chin level. REPEAT FOUR TIMES.

As you pull the elbow down, you should feel a pull between your shoulder blades. This helps to strengthen the upper back by getting one part of the body to pull against another.

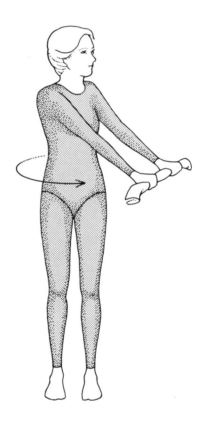

With the towel held in front of you at hip level, gently twist to the right and then to the left. Go slowly, and don't take it too far to one side or the other. We're working to keep the spine, the hips, and the waist flexible. **REPEAT FOUR TIMES TO EACH SIDE.**

Gently twisting my waist in this way really loosens me up.

Your shoulders, chest, and back all benefit from this movement.

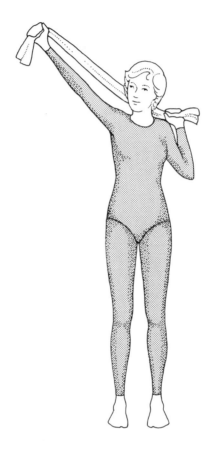

Keep your arms overhead, and slowly bring one arm down, as if you were an archer holding a bow and arrow. Reach on a diagonal, with one arm straight and the other arm bent at the elbow. The towel now is behind your head. Lift the arms up overhead, and bring the other elbow down, stretching to the other side. REPEAT SIX TIMES ON EACH SIDE.

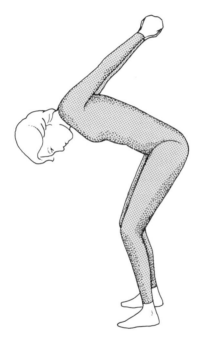

If you can, clasp your hands behind you. If you can't get your hands together, use a towel. Bend your knees and gradually lift your hands up toward your head as your body tilts forward. Here we are, bowing again! If you feel any discomfort in your back doing this, don't bend very far. Return to your starting position and repeat. REPEAT SIX TIMES.

If you feel dizzy,
stop, and only go
part of the way. This
helps to keep your
back supple and
strong.

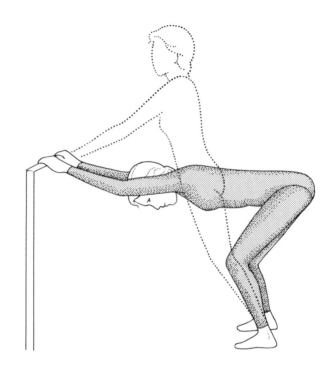

Standing about two feet away from a counter or
the back of a chair, rest both hands on the counter
and slowly bring your chest toward the floor. Your
knees are bent, and your feet are about two feet
apart. Don't force it or arch your back. You're
trying to flatten the back. If you feel your bottom
is pushing out as you come down, you're doing this
movement correctly. Then come up, keeping your
arms straight and pressing your chest to the floor.
Keep your heels on the ground so you can feel a
stretch in your calves. It's important to have a sure
sense of your balance here. Relax. Breathe normally, not thinking too much about inhaling and
exhaling as you do it. REPEAT SIX TIMES.

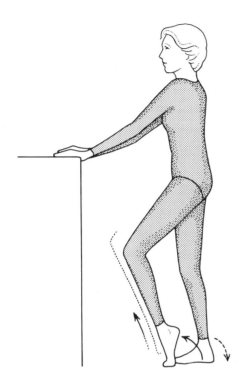

This feels almost like a foot massage, and helps your balance.

Still holding on to the counter, roll your feet, first one, and then the other. Roll each foot up, then down. When you've rolled up to the toe, push off from the floor with your toes. This movement is like prancing in slow motion. REPEAT SIX TIMES, EACH FOOT.

My calves can feel cramped from wearing high heels and walking on pavement, so I stretch them out gently like this whenever I think of it during the day.

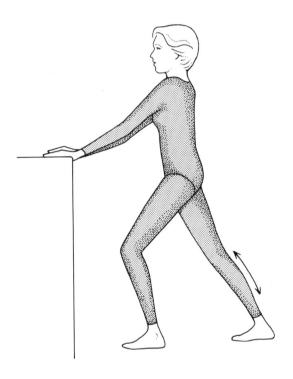

Resting your hands on the counter and with both heels flat on the floor, bring one leg about a foot in front of the other and bend the front knee. The back leg is straight. Press both heels into the floor, stretching both calves as you lean slowly into the chair, then straighten up. Make sure you don't round your shoulders. REPEAT THREE OR FOUR TIMES WITH ONE LEG, THEN WITH THE OTHER.

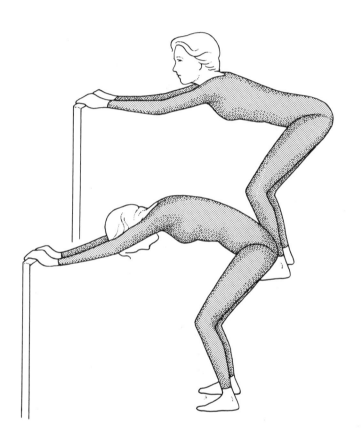

Cats seem to feel such pleasure when they arch their backs and stretch. This movement is like a cat arching.

Steady yourself on a counter or railing. Bend your knees and let your head drop down. Inhale, and lift up, letting your back arch. Exhale, rounding your back, keeping your knees bent. Inhale, arch, keeping your arms straight and knees bent. Exhale, curve your back and your hips under. Let your head relax. You'll feel this down the backs of your legs. REPEAT FOUR TIMES.

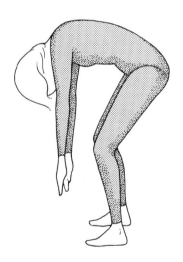

As you finish the cat arch, drop your hands from the counter. Let yourself hang with your head and arms down. Make your back slightly rounded. Now roll slowly up, pulling your stomach in and keeping the knees slightly bent. You're gently and easily rolling up, and your head is the last thing to come up.

After you've stretched and done your deep breathing, you may experience a certain clarity and feel energized. There's an effect on the brain that isn't immediate, but you will feel it.

It's a fact that your everyday motions will become more fluid if your body is limber. When you have loosened your body up by doing these stretches in the morning, standing and moving gracefully throughout the day will become easier. And chances are you'll have a more enthusiastic attitude about what awaits you in the day ahead.

3

Feeling Free

14 MOVEMENTS THAT ENHANCE YOUR MOBILITY

Throughout the day, I'll repeat many of my morning stretches whenever the spirit moves me—on the set, in the kitchen, anywhere I can stand up and move my arms and legs safely. There are many ways to relieve that tight feeling that can creep in—by raising an arm, leaning up against a door, grabbing a handle and stretching against it, swinging a leg. Those are the things that help me to get through a day. I used to find hanging was awfully useful. At each side of the proscenium stage, there are always tall metal ladders going up to the flies. In just about every show I've ever done, each night before I went on, I would climb up the ladder and hang off one of the higher rungs. It's a great feeling, just to stretch like that.

Now when I first get to the set, before I get into my motor home, I do a few stretches. The crew still look at me and wonder, What the heck is she doing? I'm just trying to get the gum running because I've been sitting in the car for 45 minutes or so on the way to the studio. If I don't do that, I feel myself stiffening up. If I'm forced to be sedentary—studying my lines, for example—I'm longing to move after finishing. I will run onto the set or run up the steps.

I spend about 20 minutes doing this next series of stretches. If I can't do this routine right after my morning stretches, I try to find another spot in my day for it. If I skip it entirely, I miss the sense of lightness and freedom that a full 20 minutes of gentle movements gives me.

Find a place at home where you're comfortable lying on the floor and you have room to stretch out fully. I lie right in the middle of the living room, on a pretty, flowered rug we had made for us in Portugal years ago.

Once you lie down, gravity isn't acting on you in the same way, so there's automatically less pressure on your spine and your joints.

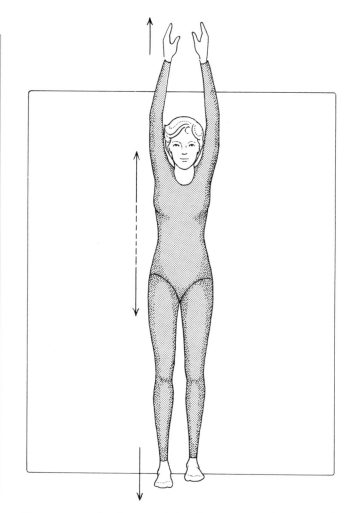

Lie on your back. Reach both arms overhead, and stretch your legs down, pushing toward your heels. Try to elongate each side of your body, from your fingertips through your toes. Slowly stretch one side of the body, relax, then stretch the other side. REPEAT ABOUT SIX TIMES.

As you finish, open the arms to the side, and bring your knees up to your chest.

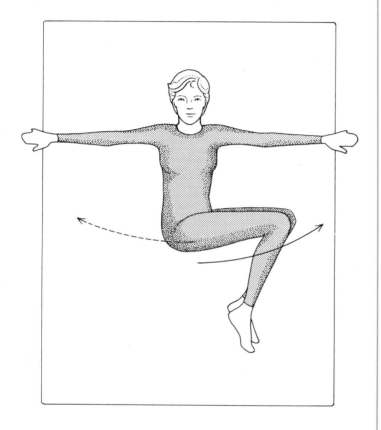

This movement loosens the back by gently twisting it, but if you have back problems, you might want to skip this one.

Lying flat on your back, anchor your body with your arms stretched out to each side and your palms down. Keep your knees together, bent up toward your chest, and roll them gently from side to side. Your head shouldn't rotate. Inhale as you bring the knees up. Exhale as you roll to the side. Don't forget to pull in your stomach. Go only as far as you comfortably can, being careful not to force the twist. After a while, you might be able to get your knees touching the floor on each side. REPEAT FOUR TIMES TO EACH SIDE.

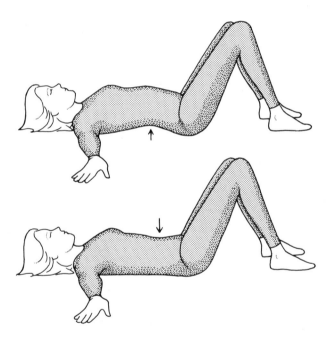

With your knees bent, your arms stretched out to the side, and your feet flat on the floor, inhale and allow your lower back to arch a bit as you roll your pelvis up toward the ceiling. As you exhale, draw your stomach in and press your lower back into the floor. REPEAT THE ARCH AND INHALE, FOLLOWED BY THE EXHALE AND PRESS, FOUR TIMES.

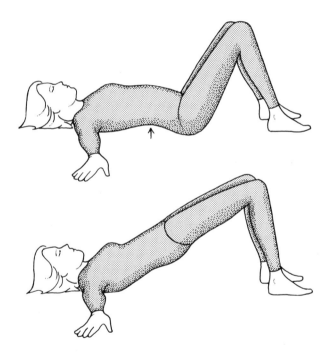

In the same position, inhale and arch your back. Then lift your hips off the floor, toward the ceiling. Hold for a moment. Breathe out as you gently roll down, one part of your spine at a time, till you're comfortably resting with your back flat against the floor. REPEAT SIX TIMES.

For the next few movements you'll need a long sash or belt, anything you have around the house that will support your leg.

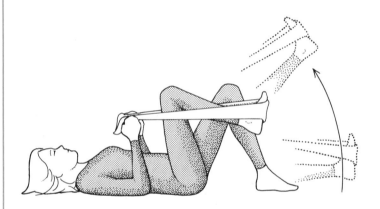

Lying on the floor, rest one foot flat on the floor, with the knee bent, and place the sash around the ball of the other foot. Bend your knee and slowly push your leg up, till it's about an inch above the floor. Then straighten the knee, lifting the leg up at a 45-degree angle to the floor, keeping some tension in the sash for support. Hold for a moment. Bend the knee and bring it in, toward the body, and down, back down to the starting position. Straighten, push out, and lift. Keep your elbows on the floor. This is a bit like a one-legged bicycling motion, but in reverse. REPEAT FOUR TIMES. This movement helps you maintain flexibility in the legs and hips.

Using a sash gives me added support in lifting my legs.

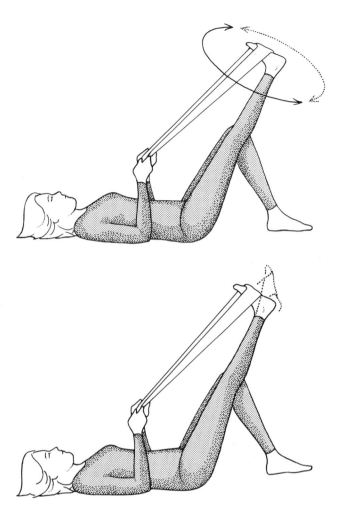

With the sash still around the ball of your foot, the knee straight, and your leg elevated, gently circle the leg, first one way, then the other. REPEAT FOUR TIMES CLOCKWISE, FOUR TIMES COUNTERCLOCKWISE. These circling movements help increase mobility in your hip joints.

Holding your foot up with the sash, point and flex, holding each position for a slow count of four. REPEAT FOUR TIMES.

CHANGE THE SASH TO THE OTHER LEG, AND REPEAT THE LAST THREE MOVEMENTS.

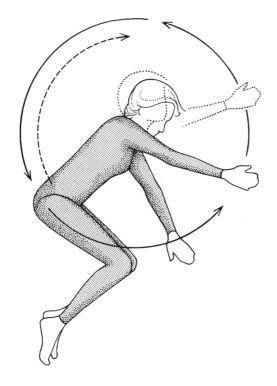

Let go of the sash, roll over to one side with your knees bent. Open your free arm and circle it around behind you, turning your head and following your hand with your eyes. Then circle your arm around in the opposite direction. Your body is rolling slightly with you. Lie on the other side, and repeat, circling in one direction, then the other. As you circle, try to keep the tips of your fingers touching the floor. REPEAT FOUR TIMES CLOCKWISE, FOUR TIMES COUNTERCLOCKWISE ON EACH SIDE.

Sit as upright as you can, with your legs straight out and a bit apart. If it feels more comfortable, try putting a small pillow under your fanny. Rest your right arm on your right leg and reach the left over your head and stretch toward the right leg. Keeping your torso stretched to the right, circle the left arm once, brushing it along the floor and then overhead. Reach both arms to the right, and then lift both arms overhead and hold. Slowly place both arms on the floor behind you and gently lift up your head and chest. Breathe in. Be careful not to let your head drop backward. Breathe out. Now do the same movement, reaching with the right arm. Hold both arms up. Bring them down. Lift up. Relax. REPEAT FOUR TIMES WITH EACH ARM.

I hold this stretch, looking skyward.

You'll need the back
of a sturdy chair for
these next moves.

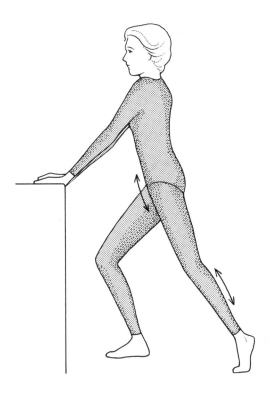

Straighten one leg behind you. Bend the knee in
front and lean into the chair, feeling the stretch in
your calf and across the front of your hip. It's all
right if your back heel comes off the floor and your
weight is on the ball of the foot. REPEAT FOUR TIMES
WITH EACH LEG.

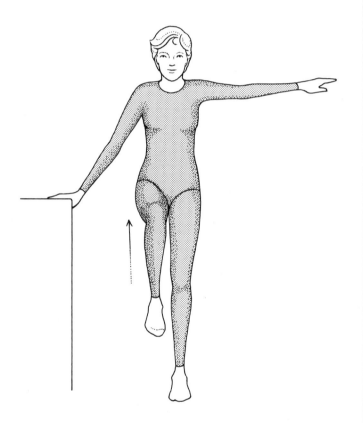

This move is for your tummy. Rest one hand on the back of the chair. Lift one leg up, bend the knee, and pull your stomach in. Hold. Release and let the leg drop. Switch legs. REPEAT TWO TIMES WITH EACH LEG.

I like this movement because it reminds me that I can exercise control over my legs, and it increases my sense of balance.

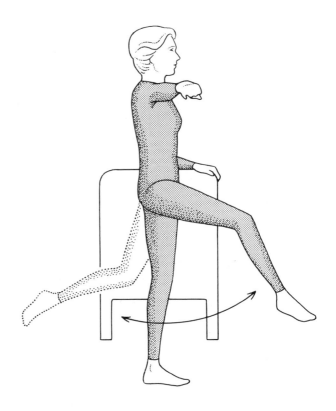

Balance yourself by holding on to a chair or a railing. Bend the knee slightly and swing the leg to the front and the back, keeping it just off the floor. Repeat with the knee straight. Just a few of these will help to loosen up the hips. WITH THE KNEE BENT, REPEAT SIX TIMES WITH THE LEFT LEG, SIX WITH THE RIGHT, THEN SIX TIMES EACH LEG WITH THE LEG STRAIGHT.

Swinging my legs reminds me how limber I really am—and how much I want to make the effort to maintain my flexibility.

Our feet and ankles
take a beating
during the course of
the day, and circling
them like this keeps
the ankle joint
flexible and gets the
blood circulating.

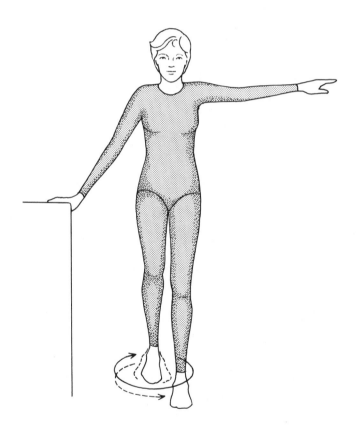

Hold on to the back of a chair. Lift one leg a few inches off the floor and circle the ankle, first clockwise, then counterclockwise. Repeat with the other foot. REPEAT FOUR TIMES EACH DIRECTION, WITH EACH FOOT.

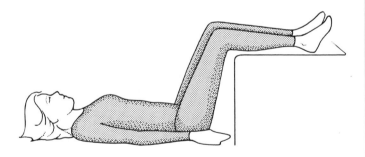

This is a great position for relaxing. Support your legs on a chair or couch. Let all your muscles go limp. Close your eyes if you feel like it, and if you nod off, so be it!

You can now create your own dance — just enjoy the feeling of moving your body. Not far from my home is a park where there are walking paths that overlook the ocean. Exercising in that glorious setting is never a chore, so one dry spring day I joined the usual complement of walkers, joggers, roller skaters, and skateboarders who flock there for their regular morning exercise. After I had walked a few good miles, I stopped to rest, leaning back against a gigantic palm tree.

I was suddenly distracted by a strange sound, a series of atonal cries coming from nearby. I looked over my shoulder and saw a lean Asian man in his fifties, facing the sun just peeking over the horizon. He was performing a t'ai chi routine on a patch of grass. His arms carved the air with graceful, circular movements as he glided from one posture to the next. I was absolutely fascinated by his concentration and the beautiful flow of his motions. It looked to me almost as if he were creating a dance that expressed feelings of strength and tranquillity.

Ever since, whenever I have the time and the inclination, I follow the stretches and gentle movements I've described with a few minutes of what I call "dancing freely." It's a special way for me to use my body after it has been loosened up. I often do it outside on our deck, where I can breathe the fresh air. (You'll need a bit of space for this.) I turn on some music that's melodic and easy and I swing my arms, stepping lightly but regularly to the rhythm. Having stretched and warmed up my muscles, my free dance improvisation feels wonderful. Oh, if Tommy Tune or Jerome Robbins were watching, they wouldn't think much of my performance, but that's okay. In fact, that's precisely the point. In these moments, I am on my own private

When I let my body move freely and easily I take advantage of all the stretching and loosening up I've done—and it feels terrific!

stage, where my memory of the man in the park at sunrise gives inspiration to my al fresco flights of fancy.

My whole dance history is based on mimicry. When I was a child I watched Fred Astaire, Eleanor Powell, Ginger Rogers—all the great movie dancers. The impression they made on me was so indelible that I found my body could literally translate what I remembered about them into movement. You can try picturing someone graceful in your mind's eye, then feel yourself moving as they do. Or simply tune in to the natural movements of your own body and let them guide you to your own choreography.

When I first began dancing as a child, the Isadora Duncan school of Greek dancing was all the rage, and we would prance around wearing these funny little tunics. But I appreciate now that gracefulness was the most important element of that dancing, and graceful movements have continued to interest me. Oh, in the sixties I rocked with the best of them, but as I grew into myself, I went back to the movements that helped me to have good posture and move as if I didn't have a hurting joint in my body, which isn't always true.

I do have some arthritis, and there are times when it hurts me just to walk. But I'm not going to let anybody know. Sometimes I even take a mild painkiller like Bufferin. Although you have to deal with the givens, I don't focus on my limitations. I make a conscious decision to ride over them, and I find that the less I dwell on them, the better off I am. I concentrate on something that will take the eye away from the problem. For example, I stand as tall as I can, and I like it if someone says, "Doesn't that woman have marvelous posture? Look how gracefully she walks!" I would much rather get attention for something positive.

Although I'll spend 10 or 15 minutes doing these free movements occasionally, just because it feels right some days doesn't mean I have to incorporate it into a regular routine. I don't set great requirements for myself when it comes to exercise. The danger of making a resolution to walk three miles a day, five days a week, for example, is that you'll overdo it and give up before the week is out, feeling like a failure. Instead of making a grand plan, I just do what I can, when I can. I believe in starting gradually with any exercise. When I feel that I can do more, I will.

But more is not necessarily always better. I think 15 to 30 minutes of exercise a day is great. If you do 5 minutes, if you do 2 minutes thinking of yourself, that, in itself, is beneficial.

In fact, if I don't feel like exercising one day, I don't. The sun is still going to rise and set, and I know I'll get back to it another day. I have no guilt hangups about skipping a day—self-reproach is dreadful. I know it's important for me to stretch, and I feel a lot better if I do it, but I am simply not fanatical about it. And I'm against moving if it hurts. If it hurts, stop.

It's very important when you don't feel well to rest. I'm not militant about exercise in that context. Rest is far better than exercise if you have the flu or a bad cold. Obviously, you try to shake yourself loose. I have to, in my business, to go to work. I get in the shower for a long time and wash my hair and I think, "Lord! I've gotta go to work." But fatigue is real, and shouldn't be overlooked. If I can, I give in to it. Rest is a great healer and energizer.

The real value of any exercise routine for me at this time of my life is its ability to help me work through the simple stiffness I often feel at the beginning of the day. My fear is that if I allow myself to remain stiff, because I don't want to feel the discomfort sometimes involved in working through it, then I will eventually and permanently become the stiff person that I am sometimes. I envision myself a bit bent, with bad posture, unable to stride out, unable to move the way I used to. That vision motivates me to do everything I can to loosen up. If you can put up with that bit of discomfort to stretch through the morning's stiffness, you'll be amazed at how different you'll feel all day, how much readier you'll be to take on any challenge.

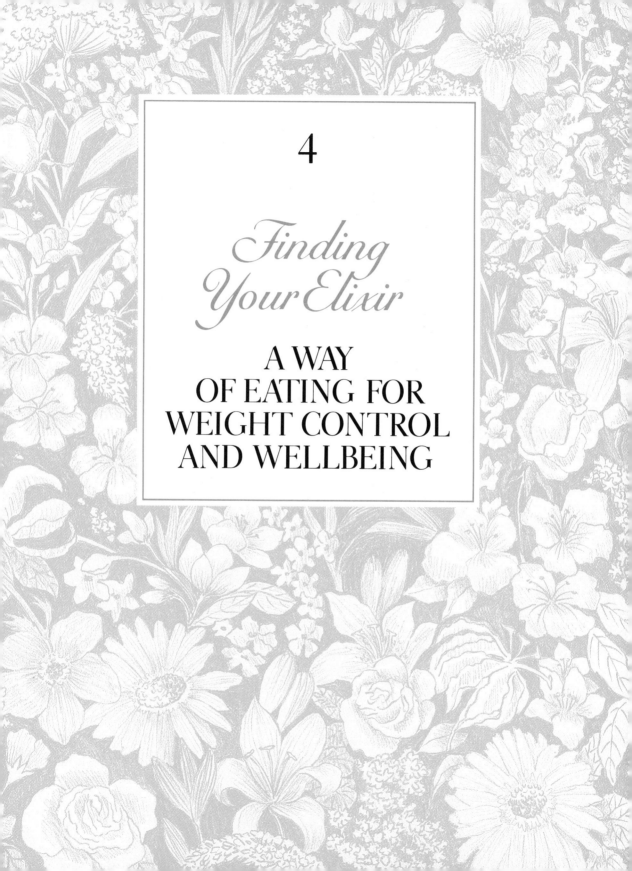

4

Finding Your Elixir

A WAY OF EATING FOR WEIGHT CONTROL AND WELLBEING

On a sunny, warm, perfect summer Sunday several years ago, my family gathered at our home to celebrate my son's birthday. Several weeks later, as I sat watching a video Peter had taken of the party, all my senses recalled that lovely day. The sweet-spicy smell of the chicken cooking on the barbecue. The delicate colors of the pots of pastel roses that decorated the patio. My grandchildren's happy shrieks as they splashed in the pool.

My enjoyment of the home movie abruptly ceased when I saw myself carrying the birthday cake out from the kitchen. I wasn't lit in the most flattering way, as I usually am in television, and I almost didn't recognize the woman I saw. Wearing a tent dress over my swimming suit and a big, frumpy hat, I was completely relaxed at the party, secure in the bosom of my family. But my smile couldn't overshadow the fact that I was shockingly overweight. I thought, "How ungainly I look, big and shapeless, with those unattractive, fat arms. That's not the woman I want to be."

I knew it was time for a change when I saw myself on that video. It was the moment of truth. Something "clicked" in my head, and I made the decision to get the extra weight off. I didn't have to lose an ounce to be professionally successful. The producers were perfectly happy with Jessica Fletcher as a big, tweedy lady. But I wasn't happy with myself.

It was no mystery to me how I had gotten up to 165 pounds. During the first season of *Murder, She Wrote,* I started to overeat habitually, nervously nibbling on snacks all day. The routine of doing a weekly television show was new to me, and I didn't know how to cope with being trapped in one place for more than twelve hours a day. In television, you often find yourself sitting a lot, between scenes. It's easy to fall into unhealthy patterns, and I did. In a short time, I was carrying around fifteen extra pounds.

For a while, I kind of sank into my expanded body. I said to myself, "Well, this is the way I am. I'm of an age now and I'm going to just stay this way." But as much as I tried to deny the need for a change in the way I was eating, I couldn't ignore the litany of physical complaints that were regularly plaguing me. When someone casually asks, "How are you?" you want to be able to answer, "Splendid!" and mean it, not think to yourself, "I've got a devil of a headache" or "My stomach is out of sorts today."

I think the worst thing about that extra weight was that because of it I began behaving differently, and people treated me in a new way. I became really too sedentary for words, and I took to moving more like a heavy person. The people around me responded by helping me up and down steps. I really wasn't accustomed to having someone extend a hand to help me up out of a chair!

The man who shopped around Los Angeles to find clothes for the show began bringing me dresses from a store for large sizes only, because he couldn't find enough attractive size 14s in the regular stores. I had never thought of myself as an overweight woman who couldn't get into a normal size 12 or 14. I really felt quite ashamed. I had been a mover all my life, and having let this happen to me was rather a horror. My self-image was that of an energetic, graceful woman, not a lumbering, dependent tub. I was not even sixty—certainly not ready to accept myself as thick and slow in a way I had never been up to then.

Seeing myself on the home video shocked me into finally taking charge of the situation. I knew I could do it. I had lost weight many times in the past. In my business, everybody whips themselves into shape for a role. With me, it had always been a matter of taking off five to eight pounds.

I had never had a real weight problem, and dieting was never a major obsession. I wasn't one of those people who was always trying new diets, repeatedly losing and regaining twenty or thirty pounds. My weight didn't fluctuate that much, and I had never gotten really huge. A few times in my life I'd notice the pounds creeping up. I'd look into whatever the popular wisdom of the time was about dieting, try some regime, lose what I had to, and I'd usually keep the weight off for a good while.

When I was in my middle thirties, for example, my life revolved around my home and my young children. I was playing a lot of tennis, so I was carrying a lot of muscle, but that wasn't all of it, if truth be told. In the process of nesting I had spread a bit, and I was wearing size 16s then. I remember my husband had to go to Rome on a business trip. During the three weeks that he was gone, I decided I would lose some weight. I dug up an entire garden—worked like a stevedore and ate very sparingly. I think cottage cheese and fruit were my mainstays then. By changing my focus from the kitchen to the garden, I got my figure back in those three weeks.

Of course, once I abandoned the cottage cheese and went back to all the foods I usually ate, it was easy to gain again. I remember Albert Finney saying to me when we were in *Hamlet* together, "You do love sweeties, don't you?" With boxes of candy around my dressing room and voluminous period costumes to hide under, I became a somewhat heavy queen. Once *Hamlet* was over and I was scheduled to go into a tour of *Mame*, I took myself in hand and banished my sweeties for a time.

I was in my early forties when I first did *Mame* on Broadway. Every night I would go back to my dressing room after the final curtain call, flushed with exhilaration from the evening's performance, to find a chilled bottle of white wine awaiting me. I could easily knock off half a bottle before going to the dinners and parties to which I was frequently invited! Doing that show, I exercised so wildly that I was hungry all the time. Not surprisingly, my costumes started feeling tight. I thought to myself, "You're blowing it, kid. Here you are, the toast of New York, and you're putting on weight."

In those days, high-protein diets were all the rage. I decided to try that quick-weight loss method, and I remember I'd have yogurt and a hard-boiled egg for breakfast and every night at five o'clock I'd eat a steak. My breath was terrible, which the diet's advocates explained was an unavoidable side effect that occurred when the body burned up its toxic fat. What malarkey! Everyone said to keep drinking lots of water to clean the breath, but it didn't help much. The pounds did come off, but I was also walking all over New York, which really helped a lot.

As I look back now, I see that whether I was crash-dieting for my work or to look good for my husband, the weight never really stayed off, because I couldn't stick with those extreme regimes for long. They were too confining. They were designed to get the pounds off quickly. Once that was accomplished, I'd go back to my usual way of eating, and the weight would creep back on.

But when I set out to make the woman on the home video a memory, it was different. I had noticed one of the men on the crew of *Murder, She Wrote*, a man about my age, who used to waddle around with a big belly in front of him. One day, I noticed he had become a thin, young guy. He had lost about twenty pounds. I asked him, "How the devil did you do it?" He told me, and I adapted his eating plan for myself. I lost the fifteen pounds in about three to four months, got my health back, and regained my sense of self-respect. And for five years, I've kept the weight off and more.

The eating plan that made a difference isn't a diet, in the way I had always thought of reducing diets. It wasn't a strange, impossibly restrictive way of eating that was to be followed until one lost the weight and then abandoned. It was a healthy way of eating that I used to lose fifteen pounds, and have stayed with ever since. When I first made a commitment to myself to change my way of eating and lose weight, I asked Peter to cooperate with me and not to force food or second helpings on me. He agreed not to make me wobble in my resolve, and I know the kind of support he gave me was an important element in my success.

We follow a low-fat, high-fiber eating plan that includes lots of fruits and vegetables, grains, and limited amounts of protein. Seventy percent of what I eat is fresh fruits, vegetables,

The vegetables I pick in my garden make the best salad. I know I'm not imagining it. They really taste better than store-bought.

and grains. I limit myself to about 6 ounces of protein a day. When I'm working, I don't vary what I eat, and that very strict routine helps me maintain my weight and my energy. I eat the same quantities from the same food groups each day. When I want to take off a few pounds, I'll cut the quantities in half or thirds, but the foods I'll be eating will be the same. (I'll have a cup and a half of salad instead of three cups, for example.) I'm not advocating that the way I eat is right for everybody. But boy, it works for me.

I start the day with a large glass of fresh-squeezed juice and a piece of melon or papaya. I always have another fruit around eleven, an apple or banana. (In England, we used to call our late morning snack "elevensies," and it was usually tea and a cookie. The English are quite clever, really, about the way they break up their eating throughout the day, and they're not an overweight nation.)

For lunch, I have a tremendous salad or a big salad sandwich. It's full of yellow vegetables, green vegetables, root vegetables, everything but the kitchen sink, all chopped in. I use a little dressing on it, usually one made with olive oil and lemon juice. With the salad, I'll eat a whole-grain cracker. Once in a while I'll chop in a small piece of low-fat cheese, and I often have half an avocado as well, in the salad or with a piece of toast.

Kitchen Sink Salad

TWO SERVINGS

½ bunch arugula, coarse stems removed
½ head romaine lettuce
½ zucchini squash
1 small crookneck or yellow squash
¼ jícama*
2 green onions
1 carrot, peeled
1 medium tomato, peeled if you prefer
1 cup cauliflower florets
¼ avocado, peeled
1 ounce slivered almonds

Tear the arugula and romaine lettuce into small pieces. Chop all the vegetables into ¼-inch dice. Add the slivered almonds to the salad bowl. Toss everything with 2 tablespoons of my favorite mustard vinaigrette (*recipe follows*), or any salad dressing you like. You really don't need to use more dressing than that, because the vegetables themselves have so much flavor.

Note: Of course, there are so many local, delicious salad greens to choose from. Experiment with them and you'll find that each new combination creates a whole different meal.

*Jícama (pronounced *hick*-a-mah) is a Mexican root vegetable with a brown skin and a crisp white interior that is always eaten raw. If it isn't available where you live, you can substitute ½ a bell pepper or a sweet red pepper.

Mustard Vinaigrette

2½ teaspoons balsamic or red wine vinegar
¼ teaspoon Dijon mustard
½ clove garlic, minced
Pepper to taste
½ cup olive oil

Place all the ingredients, except the oil, in a small bowl and whisk them together. Continue whisking and slowly pour in the oil until everything is well blended.

For dinner I'll have fish or poultry (with the skin removed, of course) or sometimes pasta with a salad. If I'm having a small piece of fish, I'll probably have as many as three vegetables with it, so it's a substantial meal. That's about it—most of the time, and certainly when I'm working.

When I eat out, I'll order my salad dressing on the side, or ask the waiter to bring me a little olive oil and vinegar. I often eat at my daughter and her husband's Italian restaurant in Santa Monica, and my favorite dish there is angel hair pasta with fresh tomato and basil sauce that I eat without cheese. I make my own version at home too.

Angel Hair Pasta with Fresh Summer Tomatoes

TWO SERVINGS

1 pound ripe tomatoes
2 tablespoons olive oil
½ medium yellow onion, sliced very thin
1 large clove of garlic, peeled and chopped fine
Coarse salt
8 ounces dry angel hair pasta, or any long, thin pasta

Blanch the tomatoes in boiling water for 1 or 2 minutes. When they are cool enough to handle, remove the skins and seeds, and cut into quarters. (I like to use Italian plum tomatoes, but any kind will do.) Heat the olive oil in a skillet on medium heat. Then add the onion and sauté until it's transparent. Add the quartered tomatoes, garlic, and salt, according to your taste. Don't forget you've probably put some salt in the water the pasta is cooking in, and some of that flavor clings to the noodles, even after they've been drained. Simmer the tomato mixture gently for about 15 minutes. When the pasta is cooked, pour the hot sauce over it and, if you like, add some fresh chopped basil leaves as a tasty and colorful garnish.

These days, it's easy to eat wisely in most restaurants, if you are selective. You can get just about anything you want on your plate if you ask for it. It can be worth the effort to ask that the kitchen go "easy on the sauce." I stay away from creamed soups and concentrate on grilled items. Of course, people tend to be so polite to well-known personalities. My daughter used to point out that when you are one, you can get anything you want. But enough people are conscious of what they're eating today that restaurants are accustomed to satisfying special requests. I know that Deirdre is very gracious. She makes a special effort so that people who watch their weight feel comfortable in her restaurant, and I'm sure many other restaurant owners do the same.

As anyone who has tried to stick to a diet while traveling knows, it takes special effort to eat healthfully when you're away from home. When I'm going to be abroad for some time, I pack a juice squeezer. Wherever our travels have taken us, we've always found fresh oranges, brought them back to our hotel room and made wonderful juice. If you don't want to look for a grocery or fruit market in a strange place, you can order fruit from room service in most hotels. But looking for a produce market or a bakery that makes whole grain bread in a foreign country can be an adventure. While you're stocking up on healthy foods for snacks, you can soak up some of the local color.

I try to stay as close as possible to my way of eating when I'm on the road, but I don't deprive myself of some of the wonderful local specialties. When we made the television movie of the popular novel *The Shell Seekers*, we worked on the Spanish island of Ibiza for a week. I didn't pass up the chance to try what was touted as the region's best paella. I just paid attention to the size of my portion.

I'm not a total saint. It takes a lot of willpower for me to resist hot buttered scones with clotted cream and homemade jam when I'm in Ireland. I don't deprive myself entirely, though. I'll have the scones, then eat just a salad for dinner. I know that it's okay to fall off the food wagon from time to time. Knowing that makes it easier to eat sensibly 80 percent of the time. It's possible to maintain a reasonable weight and still allow yourself some slips and treats. You don't gain five pounds from a single meal of high-calorie food. You're only in trouble if you follow that up with another high-fat meal, and another, and lots of snacks and rich desserts.

I went through a process of trial and error to find what would work for me, and I'm convinced that's the only way to find a way of eating that you can live with. Especially in a regimen in which the same foods are eaten often, there's no point in trying to force yourself to eat things you despise. I genuinely like the healthy foods I eat. I look forward to a nice, firm banana in the morning. I absolutely crave the crunch of a good salad if I haven't had one for a while. I have found I'm drawn to the foods that make me feel good. It might sound a bit weird, but I can get really excited about a plateful of wonderful, fresh broccoli (with a sprinkle of lemon pepper on it).

Coming to know what to avoid in my diet has been another important part of the trial-and-error process that has brought me to my current way of eating. Just by paying attention to past experience, I've figured out which foods will trigger a headache. Creamy, fatty foods, French sauces, Greek lamb—most heavy, greasy dishes slow me down and make me feel rotten. I feel so light and clear in my head when I'm not eating heavy food. I've noticed that if I eat a large amount of fresh-cooked spinach, I get a terrible headache. I remember that when I was pregnant, my doctor prescribed iron pills for me, because that was thought to be important in those days. I couldn't take them, because when I did, I got severe headaches. Spinach has a lot of iron in it, and obviously it's something I'm careful about eating now that I've identified it as a problem food for me. A lot of people have sensitivities to particular foods, but too often they choose to ignore them because they're afraid they'll have to give up foods they enjoy. Studies about foods that cause reactions in certain people are routinely reported in the medical literature and then digested in the popular press. I always pay attention to that kind of information, and have really benefited from it.

When I was trying to lose that first fifteen pounds, I was quite rigid. A sweet or a piece of cheese never passed my lips. (I didn't keep tempting food in the house, and that does make it easier. Out of sight, out of mind.) When I saw how well my way of eating was working—I was losing the pounds, not feeling hungry, and not experiencing adverse physical symptoms—my inclination was not to tamper with success. But once I lost the weight, I loosened up a bit.

If I want to vary things slightly, I increase the amount of protein I eat and cut down on my vegetables. As a rule, I'm pretty strict during the week, and I'll stray a bit on weekends. I've had to wean myself off cheese, which I love, because most cheeses have a high fat content. But on a Saturday, for example, I might choose to have a wedge of Brie with some hot, crusty French bread and chutney for lunch. It's not a binge. I'm still paying attention to the amount of fat I'm consuming, and I know that my way of eating all week makes it okay for me to have a delicious chunk of cheese occasionally.

Although I don't count calories, I've always understood the importance of food values. I know how many calories there are in a slice of bread or a tablespoon of butter. There is so much literature available on the content of food that it isn't difficult to educate yourself a bit on the subject. The way I eat I know

I'm taking in fewer than 2,000 calories a day. I'm not starving myself—that's a good amount of food, especially when it's mostly lean foods, like fruits and vegetables. As long as I keep my intake under 2,000 calories, I'm not going to put on weight, and the same is true for most people, unless they're terribly, terribly sedentary. It's only when we regularly take in 2,500, or 3,000, or 4,000 calories in a day that we get fat. So if a generous slab of cheesecake contains 1,000 calories, many of them from fat, adding that to what I normally eat is going to push my total over the top. A taste won't wreak major havoc, but since I'm a creature of habit, I've really eliminated ice cream and fabulous desserts from my repertoire.

One of the reasons I've been successful with this way of eating is I've changed my concept of what a great meal is. It was a big adjustment for me not to see my main meal as always having to be meat and two vegetables. Now I might have soup and salad for dinner, a big vegetable plate, or a baked potato with fresh sour cream and chives on it. At first, when I'd eat something like that I'd think, "Gosh, I'm doing myself out of a meal. I could have more." But why not have just what I wanted, regardless of whether it was some traditional version of dinner or not?

Now I consider a terrific meal one that doesn't make me uncomfortable, that doesn't slow me down or give me a head-ache. The digestive system changes as you grow older. I know mine has. I've become more sensitive to rich foods, and eating at odd times of day—late at night for instance—doesn't work for me. It's similar to the way in which you can dance through the night when you're young and not miss those hours of sleep, but you can't get away with that sort of thing when you're older. The body isn't as resilient. It simply won't take abuse.

Garden Vegetable Soup

SIX SERVINGS

2 tablespoons butter or margarine
1 cup chopped onions
1 cup chopped new potatoes, peeled
3 cups of coarsely chopped carrots, celery, parsnips,
*   broccoli, mushrooms, spinach, and parsley*
5 cups of soup stock
Salt and pepper to taste

Melt the butter in a heavy saucepan. When it foams, add the onions and potatoes, turning them until they're well coated. Cover the pan and cook over very low heat for 10 minutes. Add the chopped vegetables and stock and boil until they're soft, about 15 minutes. Don't overcook the vegetables, or they'll lose their flavor. Pour everything into a blender or food processor (be careful not to over-process) or through a sieve. Adjust the seasoning to your taste. This hearty soup is delicious served with a dollop of low-fat sour cream, or even plain low-fat yogurt.

I used to be quite a devotee of gourmet food. I liked to eat it and to cook it. When I was a child, cooking and food and the kitchen were very much the center of our home life. My mother was a very good cook, and my lessons in the kitchen began at a very young age. I've always cooked for my family; I've never had a housekeeper who made dinner. When we lived in Ireland in the seventies, I had the time to indulge in French cooking at

I don't ever want to be so busy that I can't find the time to make a great homemade bread.

its richest, using lots of cream and butter and cheese. Knowing what we now know about the health risks of a high-fat, high-cholesterol diet, it seems ridiculous to cook that way for myself or for those I love. Now Peter will say to me, "Try to imagine what you would like to eat, more than anything in the world." I no longer think in terms of roast pork and applesauce or duckling with black cherry sauce, or cheesecake, things that I used to love. I've had to put those things aside. I can eat a bite. I just won't eat the whole works.

Even with my new style of eating, I still get a tremendous joy out of cooking food from scratch. Although I've abandoned many of the old, fattening recipes I used to love, I still have a reliable and delicious collection of old favorites. There's a special loaf of bread that I make when I have the time. Long ago someone in the family nicknamed it "Angie's Power Loaf." It's a yeast bread, full of whole grains and the most marvelous things. I love the way it makes the whole kitchen smell.

And I've found a new challenge in microwave cooking. The microwave is marvelous for steaming vegetables without any fat. And there's less mess to clean up!

Angie's Famous Power Loaf

MAKES TWO LOAVES

2 cups boiling water
1 1/2 cups cracked wheat cereal
3 tablespoons soft shortening
2 tablespoons honey
1 tablespoon salt
2 packets active dry yeast
2/3 cup warm water (105 to 115 degrees)
4 cups stone-ground whole wheat flour
2 handfuls bran flakes
2 handfuls quick-cooking oats
1/2 cup wheat germ

Pour boiling water over the cracked wheat cereal, and stir it. Add the shortening, honey, and salt to the cereal. Set the mixture aside to cool until it's lukewarm.

Dissolve the yeast in warm water and add it to the cereal mixture. Gradually stir in 3 cups of the whole wheat flour. Then stir in the bran flakes, oats, and wheat germ. Mix all the ingredients very well, and cover the bowl with a damp cloth. Let the dough rise until it has doubled in bulk. That takes about an hour to an hour and a quarter, so I sometimes start the dough, then go out to the garden while it's rising.

When the dough has doubled, punch it down and knead it, blending in as much of the remaining flour as you need to keep it from being too runny. Knead the dough until it's fairly elastic and smooth. Then divide the dough in half. Place each half in an oiled loaf pan. Cover the two loaves, and set them in a warm place, where they will rise again. When the dough has risen, bake the loaves in a preheated, 350-degree oven for 45 minutes, or until the bread is nicely browned. For a wonderful snack, I love a slice of this bread, still warm from the oven, with some good plum jam and a cup of tea.

In adapting your own healthy way of eating, the basic information that's supported by the American Heart Association and the American Cancer Society can be your starting point: a diet that is low in fat and high in complex carbohydrates such as fruits, vegetables, and grains. You might want to discuss my basic regimen with your doctor, and find out how he'd suggest adapting it to your needs.

But the older I get, the more I realize that you really must learn about your body. The doctor doesn't know your body the way you do. Of course, he can read your blood pressure and interpret a lab report or an X ray. But you, on a day-to-day basis, are privy to more information about your system than your doctor. It behooves you to be aware, to listen, to learn, and to understand how you react to food.

Does MSG in Chinese food give you a headache? Do cinnamon or pepper send you running to the bathroom? Does an unpleasant aftertaste of cucumber stay with you hours after you've eaten one? Do you feel better the next morning if you have a big meal before going to sleep? Or do you sleep better with less food?

People who see me eating virtually the same lunch every day at work sometimes ask me if the repetition doesn't get boring to me. It doesn't. Eating healthfully has become my life-style. Oh, I like a great, tasty meal as much as anyone, but the more I eat simple, healthy food, the more I realize that no food is so fabulous that passing it up is a tremendous sacrifice. Haven't you had the experience of revisiting a restaurant you used to love in another city, and being disappointed when you ordered what used to be your favorite dish? The beef Wellington of your memory wasn't actually that incredible. More than likely, it was the company you enjoyed when you were dining, your mood at the time, or any number of other factors that made that dish loom large in your memory.

Here's how you can stay on course — most of the time. Although we supposedly eat simply to fuel our bodies, what and how and why we eat often becomes an emotional issue. There are complex feelings tied up with the self-destructive eating patterns we sometimes fall into. When I was in *Mame,* I had every reason to enjoy the fruits of my success. By letting myself overindulge and gain weight, I was in danger of giving myself a reason to feel less than I should have. No matter how good life is, when you're overweight, you lose your confidence. At those times, I remind myself that I deserve to give myself the chance to look and feel as good as I can.

Food is the center of a lot of our social lives, and it's easy to eat, just for the community of it. I have also fallen into the trap of finding comfort in food when I'm frustrated or unhappy. But I think I've finally learned to make what I eat independent of my emotional state. Experience helps. Once you've gone through the cycle of being upset and turning to food for solace, only to find out that after overeating you're still unhappy—you're just unhappy and sick or unhappy and fat—you'll probably learn not to repeat your mistakes. You recognize what you're doing and say, "No. I'm not going to fall into that trap again. I'm not going to compound my problems by gaining weight and losing my self-esteem. That doesn't solve anything."

I could never blame people who, for a period of time, find themselves in a situation in which they lose touch with their discipline. When you're in the midst of an emotional crisis, eating properly is not a priority. When someone near and dear to us is ill, for example, we cannot be so self-obsessed that thinking about our weight is important. You simply have to get through the period as best you can, and not feel guilty. We're not plaster saints, any of us, and once the crisis is over, you can take charge again, and get yourself back on track.

I hate the word *discipline*. It conjures up visions of tight-lipped denial. But there is no magic to keeping your weight where you want it. If you want to get your figure back in shape and feel sensational about yourself, it takes a little old-fashioned discipline. One trick that helps me is my visualizing technique. In my mind's eye, I see myself as I want to be, walking down the street, wearing a certain dress, looking the way I want to look. A negative image can also be a powerful motivator. If I'm faced with a plate of pastries, I only have to remember the way I looked on that home videotape, and I immediately lose my desire to sink my teeth into the gooey stuff.

I don't feel a sense of superiority because I manage to resist when others pick up that potato chip or that slice of cheesecake being offered. I only have to think about what the consequences of eating certain foods will mean to me. Just looking around at the results of other people's overeating also helps me a lot. I can visualize another person who is five times bigger than I am who does indulge in too much of the wrong foods and it helps me resist without feeling deprived. If you feel a bit deprived, hopefully that feeling of deprivation will be overcome by your sense of accomplishment at fitting into your clothes. "Wow, you look just great!" Those are wonderful words for a woman to hear.

There are great rewards to eating sensibly besides looking your best. Having a sense of well-being. Waking in the morning and not feeling sluggish. Not suffering from sugar lows or the nausea of a miserable hangover. It is so worthwhile to get rid of all the emotional baggage that comes with eating badly. It's wonderful just to shut off that boring, repetitive inner dialogue one can get involved in: "Did I eat too much?" "I probably gained two pounds from that mass of roast beef I swallowed." "Can I lose it by Friday night's party?" "I shouldn't have had that ice-cream sundae at lunch." "I'll have to do better tomorrow," etc. etc. etc. Food isn't the only thing in life. If you eliminate it as a problem, your psychological and real energy can be freed for so many other things.

Some people get into a pattern of feeling very guilty if they've overeaten. They become quite fixated on their eating adventures, and they seem to love the telling of it as much as they hate the doing of it. It's very curious. "I wish you could have seen me," they'll say. "I sat there and ate a whole bag of cookies. I could have killed myself the next morning." They create a whole drama around the simple act of feeding themselves. If you indulge in telling this sort of story, it might be worthwhile to think about what entertainment value being overweight is providing you. Aren't you getting attention for repeatedly failing to eat the way you know you should?

With all this talk about the rewards of self-control, I do want to mention that because of the tremendous Madison Avenue hype, the idea that you can't be too thin sticks in women's minds. And it's so wrong. Women don't have to be like toothpicks. Men don't want bony girls. They love zaftig women. They really do. They love curvaceous women, with hips. I remember when I lost the weight when I was doing *Mame,* the conductor said to me, "You look very slim, but, boy, I miss your tummy." He was used to standing down in the orchestra pit, looking up at me, conducting away and seeing my little belly sticking out above him.

Too often, women go overboard with dieting to compete with other women. They dress to impress other women and get thin to feel one-up on the other girl by being thinner than she is. A lot of women who think they're overweight aren't. Maybe their posture is bad. Maybe they need to firm up some or dress in a more flattering way.

When I began eating the way I do now, my goal was to get down to 150 pounds. I'm tall and broad-shouldered, and I thought that at my age, that weight gives me an ample but nicely proportioned figure. It looks well on the screen, and since the camera adds at least ten pounds, in life I actually look thinner.

By all standards of thinness, I'm not thin. I'm just regular. I have a tummy, and that's all right. Women are supposed to have that. I like having a well-defined waistline. It isn't as small as it used to be, but it's in proportion. I'm not very tolerant of lumps and bumps, but it would be foolish for me to try to live up to some artificial body standard that's right for twenty-five-year-old fashion models. How many hours a day do those girls spend in the gym pumping iron? That sort of striving for perfection has little to do with my lifestyle. I am, after all, a grandmother, and while that doesn't mean I accept looking dumpy or dowdy, I have made my peace with natural, inevitable changes that occur in the body of a woman of my years.

A Typical Day's Menu

Breakfast
- A large glass of fresh-squeezed orange juice
- ¼ of a cantaloupe and a banana or half a papaya or a piece of honeydew melon

11 A.M.
- A big red apple or an orange or a cup of strawberries

Lunch
- A chopped vegetable salad with 2 tablespoons vinaigrette or a salad sandwich or a bowl of vegetable soup
- A piece of whole wheat toast with 1 ounce low-fat cheese, like Jarlsberg or Camembert or feta

4:00 P.M.
- A cup of tea and an oatmeal cookie or a homemade blueberry muffin

Dinner
- A sliced tomato with fresh basil and a little olive oil or a mixed green salad or mushroom salad
- 5 ounces broiled swordfish or chicken or turkey
- Microwave-steamed broccoli and brussels sprouts, about 1 cup of each or any vegetable you like—carrots, turnips, baked acorn squash, lightly steamed shredded cabbage with lemon juice
- A slice of whole grain bread with strawberry jam for dessert or ½ cup tofu ice cream or a piece of fruit, such as a pear or a tangerine

These days, I'm not wild about the way my arms look in short sleeves. I have terrific muscles in my arms from gardening, but there are areas of loose skin that are just genetic. After a certain age, it's more becoming for a woman to have a little extra on her upper arms, and have a well-rounded face, rather than a face that's scrawny and gaunt from dieting, that has lost its skin tone. I have friends who live in fear of their scales, as if those inanimate measuring devices had some sort of power to affect the quality of their lives. Let's keep some perspective and remember that the goal is to be healthy and attractive.

A few years ago, I was invited to host the Tony awards. That evening celebrates excellence in the theater, and I reasoned, the theater's a theatrical place. So why shouldn't I look theatrical for the evening? I went to the wonderful Hollywood designer Bob Mackie for a gown. Everybody said, "Bob Mackie! You don't want to come out looking like Cher!" I said, "Well, there's nothing wrong with looking like Cher; however, I want to look like Angela Lansbury, but with all of the drama and excitement and that heightened, larger-than-life look that we expect from the theater." Bob Mackie really came through. He made me a fabulous slinky, elegant, feminine gown. I've never had such a reaction to a show in my entire career as I did from that appearance. The telephone calls and letters poured in. People I hadn't heard from in years called me up and said, "Good heavens, Angie, what did you do to yourself?" They were absolutely floored. They were as excited and as thrilled, and got as much of a kick out of it as I did. It really was lovely. But it also put the fear of God in me, because I thought, "Good heavens, I'm going to have to keep this up now. Usually I've been able to slink out in a caftan or something rather nice but very played down. Now I'll really have to watch my figure. Every time I step out of the box I'm going to have to come out in another sensational gown."

This is the Bob Mackie gown that knocked everyone's socks off!

After the hoopla died down, I realized that, as always, I'd fare best if I merely continued to do what felt right to me. If I believed the occasion warranted, I could go for drop-dead glamor again. Or not. And if I was going to stay in shape, it was because I wanted to, not because I felt the pressure of having to look a certain way. I think what's important isn't so different for anyone who isn't in show business. We want to eat well to look good, to be healthy and have energy, to enjoy life with those we love. If that requires eating tofu ice cream instead of the real thing most of the time, that seems a fair price to me.

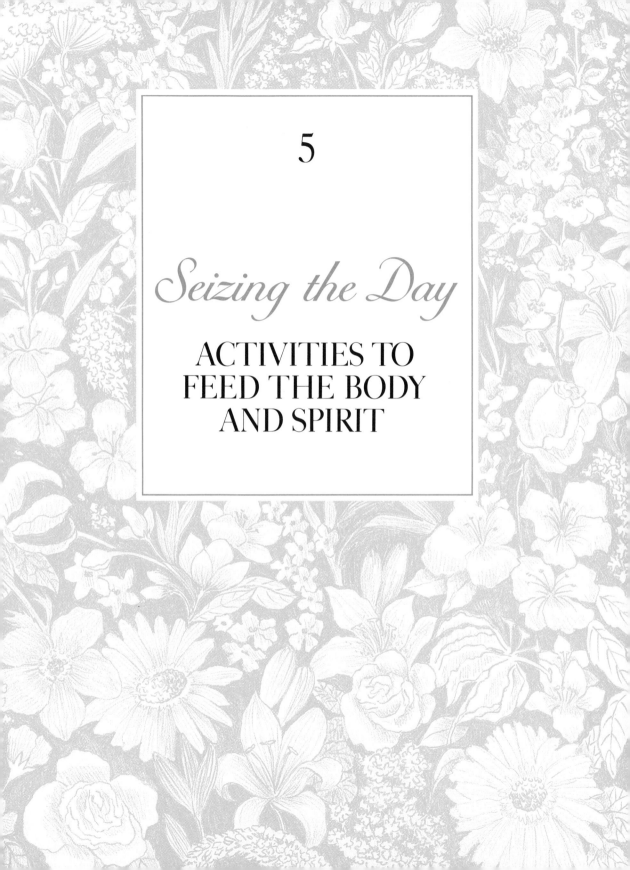

5

Seizing the Day

ACTIVITIES TO
FEED THE BODY
AND SPIRIT

"Angie, can you ride a bike?" Peter Fischer asked me.

"Well, of course I can," I told him. I wasn't about to admit to my producer, the man whose fertile imagination gave life to Jessica Fletcher, that I was incapable of doing what any school-child could do. And having committed myself to star in this TV show, I was bound and determined to do everything my spunky character would. So it was my stubborn pride that got me in this position: straddling a shiny new Raleigh touring bike on a well-manicured street on Universal Studio's backlot, with a camera pointed at me and fifty crew members looking on. I was acutely aware that if I fell on my can, there would be no shortage of witnesses to my embarrassment.

The cameraman was ready, and as I waited for the director to shout "Action," I told myself, "Of course I can ride a bike. I've done it all my life." Well, not quite all my life. I rode when I was a child, and quite a bit when we were living in Ireland. But on that warm autumn day in 1984, I don't think I had been on a bike in nearly six years!

I took a deep breath, slid my left foot from the ground to the nearby pedal as my weight shifted to my right foot and it pushed down on the other pedal. Within seconds, it felt as if my body had taken over. Without instructions from my mind, it moved appropriately, steering, pedaling, balancing, even braking when necessary. I smiled, not only because the director needed me to look cheerful in the shot, but because I could barely contain my excitement. I wanted to shout, "It's true. You never do forget how to ride a bike!"

Thinking back on it, I don't think my sense of accomplishment that day was any less than my granddaughter's the day she mastered her first tricycle. I felt strong, athletic, coordinated, ready to meet any physical or mental challenges that might present themselves.

Riding a bike is a different kind of exercise than the stretches and muscle strengtheners I showed you in the previous pages. I discipline myself regularly to do the exercises that keep me flexible and strong partially because they help me to enjoy doing a variety of things that feed my body and spirit.

There's more to a healthful life-style than bent-knee leg lifts and steamed zucchini. My personal definition of being active encompasses being not only athletic but also stimulated, busy, engrossed in all sorts of ways. My hobbies and interests keep me moving forward with enthusiasm for life and its multitude of possibilities. I think it's so important to fight complacency as we get older. Keeping my interest alive in a lot of things really keeps me youthful. Plants are meant to sit still and only lean toward the light—not people. The important thing for me is to have a purpose and a reason to get moving. I will often create that reason for myself because I know I feel best when I am interested and involved.

If I'm active, I can remain active and never run out of energy. We don't really put demands on ourselves that in any way approach our full capacity to work. Think about a day when you moved from one home to another—a day when you were in constant motion for hours upon hours. In such situations we're like soldiers on a forced march. It's remarkable how we discover reservoirs of power and energy we never knew we had. When you know the work has to be done, when you're interested, when you're loving what you're doing, when you have a sense of accomplishment, you can physically do far more than you would ever think possible.

Bike riding is one of the most releasing things you can do. Riding a bicycle for *Murder, She Wrote* reacquainted me with one of the easiest and most pleasurable activities I know, and when I am not working, I try to integrate bicycling into my routine. Of course, the car will bring me to my son's house faster, but if I'm not in a tremendous hurry, I might go the few blocks by bike.

Bike riding is like floating—the feeling of the breeze in your hair and no sound, just the whir of the bike wheels—it's a lovely sensation, and the most marvelous way of getting out in the fresh air. I'm not talking about being hunched over a European racing bike with skinny little wheels and a seat that feels like torture. There are wonderful new bikes on the market, with sturdy, wide tires, with upright handlebars and nice, wide, almost comfy seats.

Make sure your bicycle seat is high enough so when your foot rests on the pedal, your knee bends just a bit. You don't need to hold on to the handlebars for dear life. Just grip them loosely. You'll find you get less tired if you rest the ball of your foot (rather than the arch) on the pedal. Pedaling is a gentle, fluid motion that doesn't pound your joints. Although I'm never shown wearing a bicycling helmet on *Murder, She Wrote*, if I'm actually out riding on a street, wearing one makes me feel more secure. Many cities have bike paths or bike lanes, where you can cycle without worrying about traffic. You don't have to go great distances or break speed records to benefit from biking. Just enjoy it, and you'll find yourself doing it as often as you can. With a basket or pack that straps on your bike, you can use it for doing errands too.

I guess we all agree that walking is the best exercise in the world. I recently read a study that examined why people don't exercise consistently. The most common reason was that the places where they went to participate in exercise classes or to use special equipment were too far away from their homes. The study also reported that many people felt intimidated by complicated exercise equipment or fancy and expensive outfits they felt they had to wear.

Walking for exercise eliminates both those problems. When you walk near your home, you've taken away the burden of having to be at a certain place with a special outfit on in order to exercise. All you have to do to walk is get yourself a pair of walking shoes with good support, and wear a loose-fitting outfit, in a fabric that will breathe. A hat is a good idea, and it's vitally important to wear sunscreen, not only on your face but on your neck and hands as well. I'm always slapping sunscreen on. I know if I'm driving along in the car, and the sun hits me smack on the neck and I haven't put my sunscreen

Sometimes just walking around the block will perk me up, and give me energy to last the rest of the day.

on, I'll get those unattractive red or brown spots on my neck. And they don't go away so easily. It's not just vanity, either. There's the real danger of skin cancer from exposing yourself too much to the sun.

If I must do something sedentary, such as studying lines or talking on the phone, when I've finished I'll take a walk around the garden, or down the street, just to get myself moving again. Not every walk has to be a long, record-setting hike. Even a short walk can balance those parts of the day when you have to sit, and it keeps me from feeling like a drudge.

I walk at a rather brisk pace because I like the feeling of covering ground, of getting somewhere, but you don't have to go so fast that you feel out of breath. You should be able to talk easily while you're walking. Let your arms swing naturally. As your foot hits the ground, try to land on your heel, and walk in a stride that's comfortable for you. If you repeat the calf stretch I showed you just before and after taking a walk, those muscles will be less likely to cramp up and hurt you later.

If you want to lose some weight, walking regularly helps tremendously (assuming that you're watching what you eat as well). You'll find the weight doesn't just come off the legs. You'll gradually become trimmer all over. When I was a teenager going to school in New York, I used to walk from 94th Street down to 50th Street every morning. Some days I thought my nose was going to freeze off, but I loved my daily journey on foot, and I think it helped me lose some childhood pudginess as my body was changing and I was growing into my young womanhood.

Where I live now, we tend to drive everywhere. It's a very basic and well-worn saw, but I try to remind myself to walk instead of ride sometimes. I know in many parts of the country the weather can be a deterrent to walking, but even on a hot summer day the temperature early in the morning will be comfortable enough to get out in. In winter, you can find a big, enclosed mall where you can safely take a brisk walk.

Most people walk far more when they're away from home, and I am no different. When you're walking, you can drink in beautiful vistas in a way that isn't possible when you're speeding by in a car. One of my favorite places to walk is in and around Mendocino, a charming northern California coastal village that was built by whalers and resembles the fishing towns of New England. Every year we do ten days of location work for *Murder, She Wrote* there, and Peter and I always find the time to take walks along the windy headlands, where the view of the roaring, roiling sea smashing against the dramatic cliffs is breathtaking. Large seabirds swoop by, and groups of seals bark at us as they crowd on the rocks below.

I also love walking in the forest, and I've had some memorable walks in the Vienna woods. There are also heavily wooded areas near my brother's home in Vermont where I've often walked, surrounded by towering beechwoods and maples. The carpet of leaves that covers the hard ground in the fall has the most lovely feeling under my feet, even though there's something rather melancholy about the smell of the fallen leaves and the passing of summer and all its promise. I've heard that many people feel sad around their birthdays. Perhaps, since I was an October baby, the autumn is my time to be easily blue.

I love to swim to clear my head. The other sporty activity that I find both relaxing and energizing is swimming. Since it involves so much stretching, it has a wonderful way of working kinks out of the body and that tight feeling we sometimes develop. If I've been working a great deal at the studio, standing but not really moving or using my body, swimming exhilarates me—I feel all my muscles pushing against the water. I know I'm very fortunate, because I have a swimming pool in the backyard, but people who like to swim have a way of finding places to do it. Every Y has a pool, and many high schools open their pools to the public at certain hours. The important thing for swimmers of all ages to remember is to have a lifeguard or a swimming buddy around. It just isn't wise to swim all by yourself, especially in the ocean or a lake.

I don't swim laps. Once I'm in the pool, I just swim for as long as I want to, without following any prescribed program. There have been times when I've been trying to get in shape for a role that called for underwater exercises. It's wonderful what you can do in a pool that you wouldn't be able to do without the support of the water. You can extend your arm or leg without straining muscles because the water is helping you. Underwater exercise classes are quite popular now at spas and health clubs, because they offer a different way of exercising that is gentle and effective.

In the years when we had a home on the beach in Malibu, the ocean was very much part of our lives. I never tired of hearing or looking at it, of observing its changing moods and colors. To say swimming in salt water is more exhilarating than in a pool is like saying champagne is more fun to drink than tap water. Fighting the waves, sensing their rhythm, and working out some sort of rapprochement with them is an endless challenge. I never surfed on a board, but my children did teach me to bodysurf and to ride the waves on a rubber raft.

I would never deprive myself of the fun of swimming or going to the beach because I didn't think I looked terrific in a bathing suit. Does any woman feel attractive in a bathing suit,

I spend a lot of time puttering with the flowers in and around my house. I hope they give pleasure to everyone who sees them.

especially when she sees herself reflected in a store's dressing room mirror, illuminated by the sickly glow of fluorescent lighting? Like most women, I feel more confident in a bathing suit some days than others. I rely on the great-looking things you can wear over a suit, lovely sarongs and scarves and pretty cover-ups. And once you're in the water, who's to know the firmness of your thighs?

Alternative activities can help you unwind. For me, the stressful and exhausting thing about my work is being with a lot of people all day. There is constant noise and conversation, incessant small talk, most of which has nothing to do with the job at hand. I feel pressure to perform, pressure to be nice, pressure to achieve, to do all the things I want to do in what never seems like enough time. Despite the fact that most of that pressure is self-imposed, it's the sort of thing I have to get away from. I'm not an explosive person, and if I'm feeling under pressure and I don't find some release, it all tends to go in with me. I know that can be unhealthy.

So I turn to other activities that neutralize some of the stress, activities that I find very rejuvenating and revitalizing. Believe it or not, a favorite one is puttering. I putter in the garden. I putter in the kitchen. I might walk around the house and yard and pull the dead heads off flowers. I'll rearrange a bookshelf, weed through a closet, go through my spices and discard those that lack a certain youth. There's a middle ground in the mind that's almost akin to a meditative state, when my brain just sort of skittles around. It doesn't center on anything or try to solve any knotty problems. That is the relaxing mental state I sink into when I putter.

I enjoy puttering the way someone else might like putting on a marvelous outfit and going to the club to play golf. It satisfies my need for activities that are energetic, aren't necessarily strenuous, but can get my mind off other matters. And I feel my health benefits as much from puttering as someone else's might from running. Did you know that a recent medical study reported that puttering actually contributes to our longevity?

Peter will often say to me on a weekend, "Why don't you sit down and relax? Read something. Aren't you ever going to stop?" I say, "You don't understand. I'm sitting most of the week." So for me to be able to be up and around and running from room to room is the greatest tonic. On the weekends I never stop. I believe in finding reasons not to sit down, not to sit on my rear and be a couch potato. (Of course, we all do it sometimes, especially after a long, tiring day.)

It's so great to get your hands into anything... And everything. Manual work can be very calming to me too. Manual work means different things to different people (to me, gardening is certainly manual work), but all it literally means is doing work with your hands. Many people with great minds have enjoyed manual work as a release, a way for the body to nourish the brain. Winston Churchill used to build brick walls. He claimed it helped him to think. I knew a psychiatrist who used to paint walls, over and over. He had a big house, and he'd go from room to room and just paint walls. And we couldn't call him crazy, could we? He told me it was the one way he was able to clear his mind. A friend of mine, the well-known director Gene Saks, told me that when he would come home from a dreadful rehearsal and find his dinner ready, cooked by his wife, he would get tremendous pleasure out of cleaning a particularly sticky pan that was sitting in the sink. After spending a day trying to solve staging problems and telling actors what to do, he found it therapeutic to scrub the dirtiest pan he could lay his hands on.

I cleaned all the dining room windows one recent evening. I had come home from work feeling exhausted. I had spent the day working quite hard on something that was less than challenging, and I was rather bored. My mind was in a turmoil, and it was wonderful to get a bucket of hot, sudsy water and get out there and clean the windows. (That makes me sound like Joan Crawford, who was rather obsessive about scrubbing her basement floor every week.)

As you've probably guessed, I'm a bit of a do-it-yourselfer. One of my proudest achievements, an antique pine table I found and refinished in Ireland, still sits in my study. When we began settling into our Irish homestead, my son Anthony and I bought a lot of old furniture at auctions. We stored it in the drawing room, which wasn't being used, and we would labor over one piece after another, painstakingly restoring each one to its former beauty. Many days, the house was filled with the pungent smells of turpentine and linseed oil.

Eight coats of paint had accumulated on the doors of our Irish house in the 160 years since it was built. We stripped them down to the original pine, then waxed them. I remember the thrill of discovering the lovely wood hidden beneath the years of dirt and paint, then sanding it with fine steel wool till it was smooth. I haven't had time to go antique hunting lately, but I know I would take on a job like that again, if I found an antique piece that had some good wood hidden underneath coats of paint. There's a deep satisfaction you can get from doing such handiwork, and the rewards can last a lifetime.

Whenever I went to Ireland, my dual-voltage sewing machine would be among my baggage, with a huge FRAGILE sign stenciled on its crate. That machine must have been twenty-five or thirty years old when I bought it at a little shop in the city of Cork, but I used to clean and oil that bloody thing till it hummed. I made every pair of drapes for the Irish house on it. Some wonderful nubby blue, white, and tan wool tweed ones that hung in the morning room there are now in our study in California. The floor-length seafoam-green shirred curtains that were in our Irish drawing room hang in my bedroom today.

Who ever said sewing wasn't a physical activity? You really

do need to be well prepared for it, with adequate tables, surfaces, and other equipment that helps you to avoid physical strain. I've always had the odd habit of laying my fabric on the floor and standing over it, leaning down to cut without bending my knees. In the past, I've become so consumed with my task that I'd nearly cripple myself, demanding more than my back was prepared to deliver. But perhaps because I put so much of myself into such projects, the things I create become part of the fabric of my memory and my life, and I am loath to give them up. (And so I haven't!) If things are lovely, and they're made well, I think they can last forever.

Someone else might find the satisfaction I get from sewing or cooking in making pottery, playing an instrument, drawing or painting or taking photographs. There are so many things to do besides plop down in front of a television set. I'm afraid I have a rather puritanical attitude about watching television in the daytime. For me, it is simply too passive, looking into that electronic window as if there were life inside. If I want to feel happy and good, I need to feel that I'm industrious. Although I may be doing things for or with other people, staying busy is a selfish desire on my part. I know my feeling of well-being is dependent on it.

There are lots of light jobs around the house that I actually enjoy doing—mowing the lawn, or washing the car. Just think of all the bending and stretching that are involved in polishing a car. If you've always hated doing chores, think of them as exercise, because they certainly are. They are another way to keep yourself active, and while you're doing a job that needs to be done, you're doing something for your body as well. Maybe you do these things already, but you've always thought of them as simple household drudgery. Thinking of chores as exercise that's beneficial to the health of your body and mind just takes a small change of attitude and makes a world of difference.

I can think of few better feelings than getting down on my hands and knees in the garden. Do you see the terrific kneeling stool I work on?

There's nothing like the unending delights of a garden. Ever since Peter and I got married and had our first home, I've had a garden. My mother had a very green thumb, and as a small child I went into the garden with her, toting my very own trowel. In those days, there were no gardening gloves made for women, and I remember being fascinated by the old pink suede gloves my mother would wear as she weeded or planted bulbs in the rich English earth.

No matter how small my garden is, to me it is a place of tremendous peace and inspiration. I find that gardening releases my mind to drift away from whatever has been bugging me. There is so much to be aware of in a garden, such great variety, and always so many things to do. I'm continually bringing pots in and out of the house, repotting, planning, rethinking, reorganizing my potting shed. It gives me a huge sense of accomplishment to prepare the soil, to plant things and see them flourish (or not).

You can read stacks of books to learn about gardening, but the only way really to learn is by practical application and experience. I suppose I'm what you would call a cottage gardener. I don't follow a particular style. I just put things in the ground that I love to see come up. I try to create a beautiful landscape, and I want my garden to inspire feelings of tranquillity in the people who see it, just as it does for me. I'm not always wildly successful, but the pleasure I get, particularly from growing vegetables, is enormous. It feels terrific for me to be able to go out to my garden and pluck beans for dinner, then pick tomatoes and onions, chives, herbs, and lettuces for a salad. I love that sense of being self-sufficient.

Even in our apartment in New York, I had strings extended

from the kitchen curtain rods down to paper bags on the windowsills with tomatoes growing in them. I was performing in *Sweeney Todd* every night, and enjoying a thick arbor of delicious tomatoes in my little kitchen at home.

My favorite garden, of all the ones I have nurtured through the years, was, of course, in Ireland. It was a perfect, perfect garden, probably two and a half acres in all, with a big herbaceous border and a wooded area thick with mature beech trees. In spring, primroses and bluebells would sprout, bringing splashes of color into the secret garden in the woods. My Irish garden was quite wild, except for a sunken rose garden that Peter and I built and a large, walled vegetable plot where we grew blackberries, loganberries, raspberries, pears, figs—everything under the sun. As involved as I was there with the very simple, basic elements of life, I remember being thrilled by the coming of spring, when the rhododendron bushes would burst into incredible blossoms of purple, pale rose, deep pink, white, and magenta.

The garden I have now, like so many other things in our modern lives, is a testament to instant gratification. In California, you put something in the ground, and two days later it has sprouted up. (In any other part of the country, you'd have to wait through the winter to see any results.) My garden is quite small, in an area behind the house that we've terraced. Cabbage doesn't seem to want to grow there, but roses, which are one of my passions, do well. However, it isn't entirely clear whether the gophers or I will win the war of the roses that we've been waging. Like Penelope, the character I played in *The Shell Seekers*, I long to have enough space for a garden with plants and trees and grass and those lovely secret nooks and crannies that make a garden a wonderful place of mystery. I don't know where it will be, but sometime soon, I will have it.

Since my garden is on a slope, I sometimes find myself in

strange positions, with one leg stretching downhill. I can easily be stiff as hell the next day if I'm not careful. If I know I'm going out in the garden, I'll be especially vigilant about doing my stretching exercises. That's another way that my regular exercises and a favorite activity are symbiotic. I've learned that you have to be careful about trying to move big, heavy pots, or tackling a job that can be difficult and risky, like pruning. I have a lot of tools that are effective without my climbing up on ladders to put myself into a precarious position, and they're readily available at any good gardening supply store or through one of the many gardening mail-order catalogues. While I try not to overdo it, and don't do things in the garden that are obviously dangerous, all the walking up and down steps, bending, stretching, and digging constitute quite a work-out.

When my mother became too infirm to work in her garden, she began cultivating houseplants. She developed a special interest in succulents, and she had names for each of them. They were very interesting to watch, and I believe they became almost like friends to her in her last years.

My grandchildren are the greatest reason I can think of for staying in shape. Although I often putter in the garden by myself, it doesn't have to be a solitary activity. I've set aside a sort of digging area at the bottom of my garden for my grandchildren, Katherine, Peter, and young Ian, and I've bought them their own wheelbarrow and shovel and things. Young children love simply to dig and move earth and stones from one place to another. They love to run up and down the steps and explore what I call my secret garden. The children love to help, doing jobs like picking the peas and beans and ripe tomatoes, but they aren't terribly interested in the miracle of growth yet! I think we're going to have to work doubly hard, as parents and grandparents, to introduce our children to the wonders of nature and the simple things that are available to them without a nickel in their pockets. They're so taken up with their electronic gadgets.

Many of my activities on the weekend have to do with grandchildren. I would be very sad if I couldn't garden and swim or walk or bike ride with them. You never know where playing with your grandchildren might take you—down on the ground, probably. For as long as possible, I want to be in the kind of physical shape where getting up from the ground is possible without enlisting the help of a crane.

Just as there is no real right way to be a parent, it seems to me that grandparenting is a role to approach in a very individual way. One of the reasons it's so pleasant for me to spend time with my grandchildren is I look forward to introducing them to activities that are meaningful to me—teaching my little granddaughter to cook, for instance. And I'm gathering together a good trunk of props and costumes for her. She's a great one for tromping around in my shoes, wearing big earrings and hats. She certainly has a flair for the theatrical. The point, however, isn't to turn her into a little actress, but just to encourage her to play in a way that taps the creative, imaginative side of her nature. Peter is teaching young Peter some timeless games, like dominoes and chess. I suppose we've both resisted getting involved in activities of theirs that don't appeal to us. I'm not one to go to Little League games, for example, but Peter is and he thoroughly enjoys going to Junior Soccer games and volunteering for linesman's duties. The beauty of sharing time the way we do is the children get to know something about us and what we value. They learn there is a world beyond their television set and their classroom.

Being with my grandchildren is stimulating for me. It keeps me sharp to answer their questions, directing my mind into some of the things that fascinate *them*, whether it be dinosaurs or computers. In many other cultures, such as China and Israel, the elderly work in the day-care centers. It's considered a natural cycle for the old to be with the young. I heartily agree. One of the great luxuries of being a grandparent is being able to turn the children over to their parents at the end of an action-packed day. That moment makes me more aware than ever of my need for rest.

Keep your mind open and you'll never be bored. But sometimes my feelings of fatigue are not to be trusted. If I'm feeling tired, I might really be bored. While a weekend filled with activity may leave me legitimately physically exhausted, I find that inactivity drains my energy in a different way. If I'm trapped into being inactive, it mentally saps me, and I will often go to sleep, literally drift off from simple lack of stimulation.

That can happen to me at work, where I spend a lot of time waiting in my motor home to be called for the next scene. The solution I've found is to bring projects to do. I'll go through a stack of catalogues and order things on the telephone. I've found this a wonderful way to shop, without ever leaving my trailer—for things for myself or my home and garden, for gifts, or for clothes to wear on the show. I often bring needlepoint or knitting to do. I don't like being bored. So it's important for me to create a situation in which I'm stimulated, no matter what I find myself dealing with.

Perhaps one reason I don't often find myself feeling bored is that I maintain a sense of wonder about the world and keep my mind open to new experiences all the time. I'm a nature lover of the first order. I get exhilarated from discovering a new place, from seeing a vista I haven't seen before. An elegant group of nine mourning doves congregate at the same time every evening at the birdbath in my garden. I can become transfixed just watching them. I'd like to learn more about birds, when I have the time. It isn't difficult to be moved by the power of nature. Get up some morning at five and go to a scenic spot and watch the sun come up. We did that recently. I hadn't seen the sun come up over Los Angeles in years. I was absolutely staggered by how beautiful it was.

As you can see, it isn't hard for me to find new things to spark my interest. I'm always yearning to take off on the open road. Houses fascinate me, as do new people who suddenly appear in my life. I love wood, linens, antique furniture, all the lovely details of keeping house. And I love to see the changes in my grandchildren—when I can get them to myself. I know that as I decrease my work load and my leisure time expands, my many interests will serve me well.

You don't have to retire to a rocking chair and a remote control. It has been my observation that few people in my business retire well, so I'm not planning to do it. I will work up to the point when I no longer want to work constantly, and then I'll work intermittently.

The friends I've seen not retire successfully failed to anticipate what a shock to the system suddenly being inactive would be. It's terribly hard not to have a regular, preordained agenda for every day, not to have a place where you must go. Boredom, depression, and illness can set in. The statistics on the number of people who become ill months after retiring are shocking. I would be a bit afraid to retire, because I know having feelings of expectancy, an awareness of what I'm going to do next, is terribly important to me.

Nevertheless, I know I shouldn't be reluctant to retire, because retirement isn't inevitably synonymous with inactivity. I know if I stopped working, I could stay busy just by finally learning how to play, something I've neglected up to now in my dedication to my career. I'm sure it isn't too late for that. The significant thing is not to retire into nothingness. People I know who enjoy their later years have stopped working (whether by choice or not) and have begun doing something else that is meaningful and enjoyable—hopefully, more personally rewarding than their work was.

Volunteering is a wonderful thing to become involved in, because you really do find that you're needed in your community. The opportunities are legion. Make an arrangement to cook one day in a shelter. Offer your time in a hospital. If you love children and are handy, you can have a cottage industry going at home, making toys or doll clothes for children.

Many people look forward to traveling when they're no longer tied down by a job. I would love to take a tour of the great gardens of England. What also appeals to me is going to a place I've never been and staying awhile, somewhere like Tangier or Marrakech, parts of the world where modernity has only slightly encroached upon tradition. (Of course, traveling is a good reason to stay in shape. It's difficult to enjoy a trip if you can't climb stairs or walk comfortably.)

In the summertime, I see older people all over America, traveling in groups. They have conquered what can be two of the big negatives of aging: inactivity and loneliness. Especially when you are no longer going to a job every day, it's absolutely crucial not to be isolated, to stay in touch, to nurture a network of friends with whom you maintain a relationship of mutual support.

I don't see how you can be lonely if you have interests. As soon as you join a group that plays cards, or gets together to discuss books, or plans outings to the theater or museums, you have saved yourself from the kind of withdrawal that can be so unhealthy. In most parts of the country, there are wonderful adult education courses specifically offered to senior citizens. After a lifetime of devoting so much time and energy to a job or raising a family, what a treat to be able to devote time to expanding your mind, learning more about a period of history that always fascinated you or exercising a long-dormant talent for interpreting poetry, or even playing the piano.

Recently a friend told me about a marvelous organization, Elderhostels, which presents weeklong courses on college campuses all over the world to groups of retired people. She showed me the catalogue, which offers an enormous variety of seminars. She's taken classes in everything from Far Eastern religions and outdoor cooking to the history of the Civil War and classical music of the twentieth century. And she's made many new friendships with people from all over the country with whom she continues to exchange letters.

Not long ago I was reminded of the necessity to seek new friends when I was called upon to reminisce about Bette Davis at a memorial service. At first, I was surprised that I was chosen to speak, because I didn't know her nearly as well as many other people she had worked with. We'd only met about ten years before she died, when we were both cast in *Death on the Nile.* But so many of the people who were close to her are gone now. When you are one of a generation that is thinning out, and the ranks are becoming more and more slender, that can be depressing, especially if you feel that the younger people around you haven't shared your experiences and don't understand your language. That's why it's so important to cultivate younger friends whose outlook you enjoy, and who value you. When you do that, you are maintaining an involvement with whatever is current.

My dear friend Mildred Knopf is ninety-two now. She told me that throughout her adulthood, she made it a habit to make friends with younger women. Most of her contemporaries are gone now, but she has friends in their forties, fifties, and sixties. Those are the women who are around her today, and they appreciate that she still has a great deal to give and to share. I know that's how I feel.

My friends who have been widowed also make the best adjustment if they don't retreat. They stay involved and active and keep the lines of communication open with the friends who were in their lives when their husbands were alive.

If you take an activity that could be ordinary, and turn it into something special, you'll benefit. As much as I enjoy keeping busy, I know that stimulating activities mustn't always make me feel like a whirling dervish. In fact, I'm a great ceremonial person, and I get a great deal of satisfaction from simple, calming rituals that, with their qualities of familiarity and grace, enrich my life each day. I might be out in the garden for hours, but, around four-thirty or five, I come in, set a tray with freshly brewed tea and a cookie or biscuit, and bring it out to wherever we decide to sit. Left to his own devices, Peter is definitely a cup-in-the-hand kind of guy. But he's always so glad once we've had tea together. It's a great pick-me-up, and it keeps me from being so hungry for dinner.

Peter and I spend special time alone together each afternoon.

I have a special collection of teacups that I've acquired over the years. Some were gifts, some lucky finds when I was traveling or working on location, some remnants of old sets of china. One day I might use a dainty pastel Meissen cup that was my sister's favorite. The next day I'll be in the mood for a big, bowl-like peasant's cup I brought back from Ireland. Each has the power to evoke an atmosphere and a time and place in my mind.

I think little and big ceremonies help us. They remind us that some things never change, that we can always re-create special moments when we feel the need. We deny ourselves so much without even realizing it. Grabbing a handful of food out of the icebox and stuffing it into your mouth, or eating fast food out of paper bags does not contribute to the quality of life in any way. If you're going to eat a low-calorie meal, make it the most delicious-looking thing. Take care in preparing it. Sit down in a pleasant place. Set the tray. Give yourself the possibility of enjoying the moment by taking an activity that could be mundane and fashioning it into a pleasant ceremony.

I make a special ceremony of getting ready to take a lovely, relaxing bath, with wonderful soft towels and fragrant oils, even scented candles and soft music if I really want to go for it. After a soothing bath I feel a renewed sense of beauty and femininity.

To preserve my energy I've learned to catnap. I'll usually take a brief nap at lunchtime, only ten or fifteen minutes. That can be very rejuvenating, and can make all the difference in how I'll feel through the afternoon. If I'm going out for the evening, I'll nap for a short while before getting dressed. I know lots of people take catnaps. But I feel there's a real difference between nodding off while you're sitting in a chair and making a conscious decision to treat yourself to a nap. Lie down, take off your shoes, maybe even some of your clothes if they're at all binding. Cover yourself with a cozy afghan, rest your head on a big fluffy pillow and commit to the idea that you are taking a break in the most comfortable possible way.

It doesn't make sense to me to care for my body and watch what I eat, then to neglect another important part of me, my aesthetic sense. Sometimes I feel as if the way I create my favorite ceremonies is a demonstration of advanced puttering. But I know my thrust in life is to surround myself and the people I love with as much beauty as I can. That's what it's really about.

My dear friend Mildred Knopf made this magnificent family quilt for me, which hangs in our hallway.

Family is the single most important unit of comfort that we have in our lives. I'm not alone very often, but sometimes Peter will go off with our son David on a weekend, to a car race or a football game. I find I'm subconsciously thinking all day about the ceremony of the reunion. I'll plan a great meal, so the extra effort I put into creating an atmosphere will make them feel good about being home. Taking extra care in the way you do things is so important to a relationship, and to making the people you care about feel wanted.

My kids used to get annoyed with me because I would set up these ceremonial meals and demand that they be there or that they put on a clean shirt and come and sit down at the table. But I fuss the way I do because I want home to be a special place, not just somewhere we sleep. I think they've finally come to appreciate most of my ceremonies. Now, with my grandchildren, I think it's important to continue them because I know our family occasions will stand out in their memories. My hope is that each generation gains a sense of identity, a feeling for who we are and where we belong from the special times we share together.

Bringing my family together in my home has been one way I have transcended the "empty nest" feeling that so many people experience. About ten years ago, we sold our home in Ireland, and Peter and I rented an apartment in New York. For the first time, we were creating a home for just the two of us, with an extra room for if and when any of the kids came to stay. After going through a period of being terribly aware of their absence, I came to realize that my kids are always going to be in my life. When they leave the nest you're relieved of the day-to-day concerns—have they done their wash or what are they going to have for dinner? But you never, ever lose the thread of interest and involvement in their lives. Their happiness, their adjustment, their success, their failures, are very, very much something you live with. If you can feel that they're still with you, in just a different way, the feeling of loss is tempered. I believe strong family ties should be nurtured and encouraged even after the children have left home to strike out on their own.

I'm a great one for holidays. The first Thanksgiving I ever

celebrated was in New York, when I had just come from England. From that time on, I thought, "This is a great celebration. I'm going to sic this on my family, and friends, and anybody who's not in their own hometown." I still plunge into Thanksgiving preparations with great enthusiasm. In certain circles, I am quite known for my giblet gravy.

I always make a big Christmas dinner and decorate the house for the holidays. I've imported a British tradition by celebrating Boxing Day, the day after Christmas. In England, on Boxing Day all the tradespeople who deliver goods and services to you during the course of the year come to call. They're given what's called a Christmas box, which is a form of gratuity. I enjoy having family and friends to an open house on Boxing Day. I make all the food and serve proper English tea, and someone invariably winds up sitting at the piano, playing carols.

I think a lot of the little ceremonies that we like to indulge in are really throwbacks to childhood. Mine are. They are reminders of my mother, and the way that she and my Irish grandmother did things. I remember the cakes my English grandmother would make with spun-sugar violet decorations on them. I've spent days trying to find those sugar violets, because it was important to me to re-create those magical cakes. I feel secure and comfy when I treat myself to that lovely cup of tea in a thin cup with a good cookie. It's as if I were going back to the security and comfort of being a child. I'm surrounding myself with a sense of coziness and being cared for, even if I'm caring for myself.

People who say they don't have time for such ceremonies don't feel they need them, I suppose. Perhaps, sadly for them, their childhoods don't bear close scrutiny. For most people, the lucky ones, childhood was a terrific time, and being mature doesn't mean that you have to let the memories go.

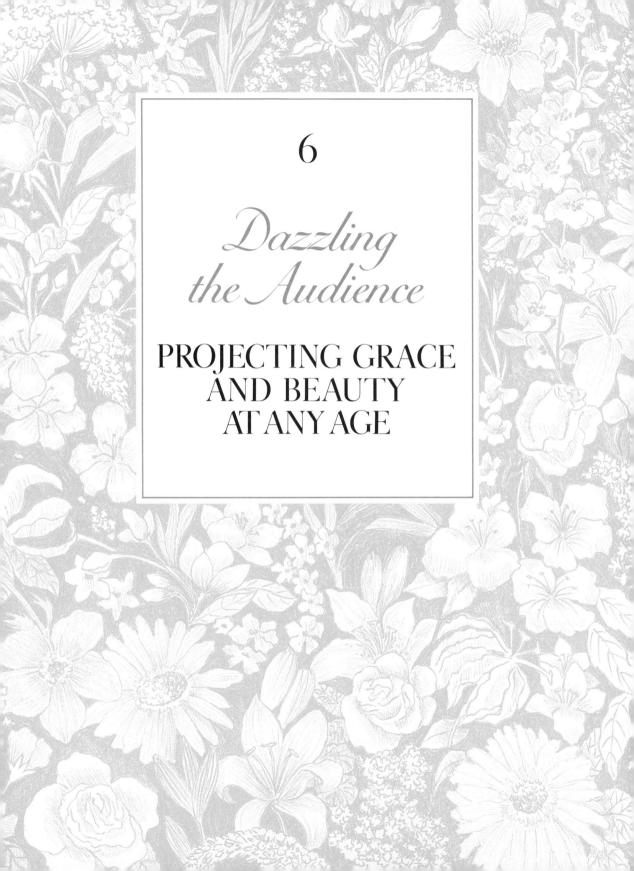

6

Dazzling the Audience

PROJECTING GRACE
AND BEAUTY
AT ANY AGE

I woke up early that muggy spring morning in 1965 and looked out on Central Park, spread like an enchanted oasis below my hotel room window. I thought about the important day ahead while I drank in the beauty of the park in bloom. I would be meeting with the producers and director of a new musical based on the hugely popular Patrick Dennis book *Auntie Mame*. I had read the script and was absolutely enthralled. I knew that this part embodied everything that I wanted to play onstage and had never had the opportunity to do anywhere—not on film, for television, or in the theater.

I knew I would have to show the people with the power to hire me that I could be Mame, that I *was* Mame, the wild, larger-than-life woman with the unconventional attitude, expansive heart, and indomitable spirit, who had captured the imagination of millions. I had been thinking about Mame Dennis for days. I loved her spontaneity, her sense of humor, her strange blend of sophistication and naiveté. She had a distinctly feminine charm and great New York style. There was no doubt about it. Mame was a terrifically glamorous woman. I knew that if I was going to be Mame, I would have to bring all the elegance and fire I could muster into that meeting.

Lauren Bacall, Lena Horne, Doris Day, and Judy Garland—who all wanted the part as much as I did—weren't going to their meetings with the producers hiding their lights under any barrels. And, I decided as I bounded toward the shower, neither would I.

Even experienced people in show business make the mistake of thinking an actress is actually like the part they last saw her portray. Four years earlier, I had been nominated for an Academy Award as best supporting actress for playing Laurence Harvey's mother in *The Manchurian Candidate.* That role was the pure crystallization of evil, so I didn't think there was much danger of anyone thinking I was like Mrs. Iselin. But they might believe I was as old as she. In fact, at thirty-seven years of age, I had been cast in that movie as the mother of an actor who was thirty-four! *The Manchurian Candidate* certainly wouldn't make anyone think of me as New York's most lovable, madcap aunt.

The composer of *Mame,* Jerry Herman, had seen me on Broadway in *Anyone Can Whistle,* a musical that closed, ignominiously, after nine performances two years before. I knew he believed in me, even though I hadn't established a big name on Broadway at that time. But it was up to me to win over the others.

In order to do that, I knew I would have to give the theatrical illusion of glamour. I would have to project it. I knew I could do that because that's what acting is. And I had envisioned myself playing just such a role—singing, dancing, and being a memorable leading lady.

So, playing the role of an enthusiastic and highly desirable actress, I strutted into the Broadway Theatre wearing a favorite white linen suit with a short, double-breasted jacket and a pleated skirt just short enough to show off my legs. Every cell in my body felt charged with electricity from some source within me. The suit, my energy, my determination, I suppose even the aura of confidence and pizzazz I enveloped myself in that day all contributed to making it a smashing meeting. I went back to my hotel room secure in the knowledge that it had absolutely gone as well as it could have.

But the producers were agonizingly slow to decide on their star. I stayed in New York about ten days, feeling more and more discouraged when no word came on *Mame*. Finally, I let them know that I had to return to California and I had to have an answer, one way or another. I was packed and ready to leave for the airport when Jimmy Carr, one of the four producers, came to my hotel. "I have the honor of offering you the part of Mame," he said, his pleasure evident in his smile. I was ecstatic. I remember flying home in a shaky old Constellation, feeling totally overpowered with excitement, a feeling that was completely appropriate and even prescient. Playing Mame on Broadway, later in Los Angeles, and on tour turned out to be everything I hoped it would be and more.

You don't have to be an actress to project glamour. I always knew that I could be whatever I wanted to be. My experience with *Mame* in New York confirmed for me that I was very much in control of how people perceived me. I got the role because, as an actress, I succeeded in projecting Mame's qualities in my audition. And then, after I had been playing Mame for a while, the oddest thing happened. Having just passed forty, I began to be considered a glamorous woman off the stage as well as on it, for the first time in my life, simply because I was projecting more confidence, femininity, and sex appeal than I ever had before. It was so simple, and is eternally effective: If you think of

When I did Mame *I felt like the most glamorous woman in the world.*

yourself as attractive, and you behave as if you are, then you will be seen that way. I think women who are not actresses can learn to emit a sense of charm, health, energy, intelligence— all the qualities that are desirable in a woman. And that doesn't have to change a whit as you grow older.

I know some women think that a benefit of aging is that they can graduate to a state where they no longer have to actively cultivate their femininity and attractiveness. I don't agree. I've never felt that presenting myself looking as good as I could was a burden. It was a reflection of my feelings of self-respect, and something I wanted to do for my husband and family. After the first season of *Murder, She Wrote*, the press began writing a lot about Jessica as a role model for mature women, citing her behavior and her look. In truth, I think we can all be role models for our younger friends and relatives. We demonstrate, by example, the importance of a woman's projecting beauty and grace.

Many older women are tremendously attractive, and they continue to be physically attractive to men. It has very little to do with their having big busts or a tiny rear that's like a teenager's. Half the time, these women are not even very beautiful, in a conventional sense. But a woman who has maintained her appearance over the years has usually put some thought behind it. Her own awareness of what she has achieved, her self-confidence and self-acceptance, contribute to a presence that is compelling. It isn't that she looks great *despite* a few creases on her face. Every laugh line is a tale, each wrinkle holds a secret.

There is an inevitable evolution to a woman's looks, and although Americans have long been accused of equating youth with beauty, I think the unrealistic standards that bedeviled us for a while are changing. We are coming to appreciate each age of womanhood for its special qualities. If youth is aglow with perfection and coltish enthusiasm, maturity brings with it an aura of womanliness and calm, a knowingness that is magnetic. The woman who tries to deny the changes time has wrought is not trusting that her natural qualities will shine through. We've all seen women who cling to styles, hairdos, and makeup that flattered them when they were thirty-five, but are simply inappropriate at sixty-five. The body changes, and we can't ignore that.

When you stand tall, everyone will notice you. In the theater, an actress often has to appear beautiful (or the opposite) to members of the audience seated so far from the stage that they can barely see her face. So we've always known that the entire body must help express our feelings and attitudes. I'm reminded of the devoted but ugly daughter in Chekhov's *Uncle Vanya*. Although she explicitly describes herself as plain, she certainly need not be played by only homely actresses. An actress in that role "acts ugly," and her body language conveys not only her physical unattractiveness but what it has done to her spirit.

Even in daily life, we often illustrate how we feel with a movement. I know I do. As I say, "Won't you come into my parlor?" I think of myself as welcoming, and my body can illustrate that for me. With my arms open, I give the appearance of being inviting. This technique of physically demonstrating a feeling can be conscious or unconscious. Without even realizing it, people who don't like themselves often slump and move awkwardly. If you become aware of how your body communicates how you feel, you can make beneficial changes.

Let's face it, what we are all trying to do throughout the day is keep our heads above water. If we can keep our necks up attitude and my posture to whatever part I was playing, the basic stance I strive to maintain is tall and graceful, elegant, if you will. How I hold myself affects how I feel. If I move with purpose, energy, and pride, then I internalize those qualities.

When I'm on the set, even if a camera isn't pointed right at me, chances are someone is watching me. So I simply won't allow myself to stand with my stomach sticking out or my shoulders slumped down. Think about what you do when someone's about to take your picture. You pull your shoulders up, elongate your neck, straighten your back, suck your belly in. Now try standing that way all through the day.

When I stand erect, I can give the appearance of vitality and strength. But the truth is, that is sometimes an illusion. I tore a tendon while dancing in *Mame*, but I had to keep performing, while taking cortisone. All real dancers have injuries, and they work through them. I was no exception. I couldn't stop. I was out for two performances, I suppose, and then I was back onstage again, doing a modified version of my dances. I started favoring one hip, and in doing that I created a situation that nurtured spurs, and heaven knows what else. To this day, the hip is crummy, to say the least, and often very stiff.

When I get up in the morning, sometimes I can hardly move one leg in front of the other. There are days that are better than others. There are days when it will just lapse on me—I'll get up and my leg will go out from under me. I can massage it quite strongly, and that helps, but the best thing I can do is keep it as mobile as I possibly can. Nevertheless, it limits me in that I can't really jog anymore. I can't suddenly get thrown into a position where all my weight is on that joint, as one might playing tennis. Jerking and swiveling movements are hard for me.

But I am not interested in becoming the victim of my out of our shoulder blades, we can rise above the garbage that's around us—head and shoulders above the inevitable petty aggravations. If our bodies communicate and demonstrate warmth and strength, perhaps we will have the power not to get bogged down by some of the cares and problems of everyday life. If you're in line at the supermarket, where everyone else is sunken into themselves, and you come sailing through with a great deal of presence, you're going to be through the line and out the door before you know it.

I think posture and bearing are very important to a woman's ability to create an illusion about herself. Some women sort of give up. They see themselves as dumpy or awkward and they tend to play that role. They might admire women who are elegant or those who have a lot of style, but they don't think they can achieve that kind of appearance. They can, if they take advantage of the simple truth that posture is an essential element of a woman's attractiveness.

Good posture should become second nature, but you can really never take it for granted, particularly as you get older. I'm five feet eight, and I was always one of the three tallest girls in my class. I played basketball, I was a high jumper, and a pretty good runner. My tall friends and I thought of our height as a plus for sports, until we started looking at the boys. In our gym class at school, we were taught always to bring the shoulders back—round shoulders were deeply frowned upon. I think that stuck with me, even through the period when, at sixteen, I was starting to work as a professional, and I slouched a lot because I felt a bit conspicuous being tall. It seemed there weren't many tall men around. So I learned to hip slouch and shoulder slouch. When I met my husband, who is six feet two, I knew I'd never have to slouch again, and I never have.

I'm so aware of my posture all the time, because it's part of my job to be. Although I have always adapted my physical aches and pains. I know what I can and can't do, and I just don't make a big deal about it. I believe in not dwelling on my physical limitations. If I do, I know it becomes obvious in the way I move and look.

Clothes make the woman, the old saying goes. How I stand and move is the foundation of how I look, but everyone knows there's more to a finished presentation. The clothes we choose tell the world that we care about making the most of ourselves. As an actress, I was never very vain. I usually cared less about how I looked or what I wore than about submerging myself in a character. With hindsight I see that I often went way overboard in frumping myself up. When I played Miss Marple in *The Mirror Crack'd* in 1980, I got myself up looking like an eighty-five-year-old woman. I didn't have to do that. It was a big mistake. I learned from experience that many people think that if you come out looking like a frump, you are a frump.

In the years that I've been playing Jessica Fletcher on *Murder, She Wrote*, I've received a tremendous amount of mail about what I wear on the show. At first, Jessica was a bit hidebound, nearly dowdy. But when we thought more about Jessica's character, we recognized that she was a woman of taste, an educated woman who traveled a great deal. She was current, with a very modern outlook. Her clothes needed to reflect that.

So we smartened her up, and the viewers loved it. One of the things that made Jessica endearing to people was that she took care of herself and she looked terrific, most of the time. She didn't dress down to her age. She wasn't ridiculously trendy, but she had a lovely kind of youthfulness about her that was exciting and very heartening to a lot of women who perhaps had set aside the idea that they might still have that quality in their look. She dressed in a way that made sense for a woman who got around, and that made a lot of people think twice about putting limits on their activities or on what they could wear at a certain age.

The person you present is the person your audience sees. If a woman wants to maintain her feminine appeal, she must think about what she's putting on her back. I'm always surprised when I see a woman who could be nice-looking wearing clothes that are unbecoming, that emphasize her less attractive features. It's worthwhile to learn enough about yourself not to make those dreadful mistakes. A full-length mirror, honestly confronted, can be a great teacher.

Luckily, we get a tremendous amount of help these days. There are so many different kinds of fashion. In the many catalogues that regularly land in my mailbox, I see so many different types of clothing available, and none of them really follow the current high fashion. I think the clothes around are very wearable.

It is possible to train your eye to recognize what works well for you. Every week, the costume designer brings me a selection of clothes he has gathered from "Jessica's closet" and the stores, from which we glean the four, five, or as many as eight outfits I'll need to wear for one show. In the process of trying on a variety of styles, I've learned a lot about what I can and can't wear. Even if you intend to buy only one outfit, it can be worth the effort to try on a dressing room full of possibilities.

Through trial and error, I've determined that big, baggy clothes just aren't for me; they make me look like a sack of potatoes. Shorter jackets with a waist work better than long, straight, boxy ones. Put me in a full skirt, and I look much bigger than I am. A skirt that's fairly fitted through the hips and flared at the bottom is more becoming.

I feel my best in very classic styles, and they seem to be ageless. (They're also good buys because classics really never change.) For me, the simpler, the more tailored, the better. American designers are masters at creating sportswear—jackets, sweaters, blouses, trousers, and skirts—that have a timeless ease about them. These basic designs are interpreted in all price ranges. But I've always been a believer in having fewer things to wear, as long as what I did have was absolutely the best quality I could afford. There's just no substitute for good natural fibers. A soft cotton, good wool, and real linen hang on the body in a way that synthetics just can't imitate.

Not long ago I went to a cocktail reception, and one of the

loveliest (but not youngest) women there was wearing a beautifully cut pair of black wool crepe pants and a white silk blouse with a pretty belt and some classic, very understated jewelry. She had a nice figure, a great haircut, and good posture and to me she looked absolutely elegant. Her outfit would have been in style five years ago and it will be five years from now.

Colors are terribly important too. They can really enhance a woman, or cancel her out. I've seen women with gentle features and soft coloring who wear very harsh colors or patterns. All you see is the pattern and you don't see the woman. I prefer dark colors, navy and burgundy and rust, but I've found I can also wear far brighter colors than when I was younger. I can wear red now, which I never could before. I think it's because my hair was a rather mousey blond for years. Now it's a more delicate beige with silver threads (I color and cut it myself), and people compliment me when I wear red. As your skin and hair color changes, you need to reconsider some colors you might have thought weren't flattering to you.

The Way We Wear Cosmetics also changes as we age. In the 1950s we all used heavy foundation makeup, from the moment we stepped out the door in the morning. The swing to the natural look in the sixties gave us a break from all that, and helped women tremendously. Now I put as little on my skin as I can possibly get away with, even for television. Less is more as you get older. If you're wearing colors that enhance your skin tone, you need less help from your makeup. When I'm working in front of the camera, I wear a rather neutral lipstick that seems to go with everything. It's a rose that picks up whatever I'm wearing.

My first job in California was at a department store, where

my mother and I got Christmas work. I was a Christmas box wrapper, and then I was promoted into the cosmetics department. I was still in my teens, and because of my English complexion, I got a lot of nice compliments. The interesting thing was, all I used on my face was a cream that I bought at the corner drugstore. I always felt like a total traitor to the cause if I told this to customers that, because I was supposed to be trying to sell Helena Rubinstein, or something like that.

To this day, I know the less junk you put on your face, the better. I think the key to my having maintained a fairly good complexion over the years has been keeping the skin clean. It's a very basic rule, but it's true. I do the simplest possible skin care. I take my makeup off with baby oil and lots of tissues. I remove my mascara with hot water. I don't use waterproof mascara because it's too hard to get off and I find it breaks the eyelashes. At night I use an inexpensive night cream. I use a moisturizer during the day. I've never felt it was necessary to plunk down a bundle of money and buy a whole cosmetic line to achieve a good complexion. I knew I was born with pretty good skin, and it only made sense to do what I could not to ruin it.

There came a time when plastic surgery seemed a reasonable option for me. Although I wasn't dissatisfied with my complexion, certain other physical changes began to affect how I felt about myself. I knew I didn't have to settle for that. I wanted to take action, and so I decided to investigate the possibility of plastic surgery. I wasn't trying to look or feel thirty when I wasn't. But I wanted to be the best fifty, or fifty-five, or sixty-two-year-old I could be.

We'd all love to be natural beauties, but we're not. As an

Isn't it fascinating to watch how we change our style over the years? Here I am at different times in my life—from the forties right up to today.

adjunct to keeping our faces pleasant to look at on television, in my profession we sometimes have to seek help.

Cosmetic surgery has been used by women in the theater since time immemorial. I know it's still a little controversial, but the audience that admires how a great many older performers look shouldn't be so naive as to think that it would be possible for them to maintain their looks without the aid of plastic surgery. In the 1920s and 1930s actresses had face-lifts, as did society ladies. Years ago, the technique of face-lifts was quite primitive. It was as if they put a sling under one's chin (or chins) and lifted everything up.

Now the techniques have been refined to a degree that is extraordinary, and plastic surgery is available to everyone who can afford it. Nevertheless, it's not something to go about carelessly. I've seen some terrible mistakes that have been made. I'll look at a woman on television and think, "How could that woman, who knows better, have gone and done what she's done to her face?" On the positive side, a friend of mine had a tummy tuck, and she went out to dinner that night, looking well and feeling terrific.

As I got older, I noticed that my neck became broader and wider, and I began to lose my chin line. When you lose your chin line, you tend to look heavy, especially to the camera. When you get your chin line back, you're halfway home. My feeling was, if I could get help by putting myself in the right hands, then why not? I had surgery on my neck back in 1976, and again in 1987. (You figure it has to be redone about every ten years.) I'm not entirely thrilled with the way the skin around my eyes looks now, but so much expression is revealed through the eyes that I'd hate to tamper with that area.

I'm certainly not out to completely revamp my appearance. When I chose to have plastic surgery, my goal was to bring how I looked back in line with how I felt. That was accomplished, and more. It's the most uplifting and wonderful thing to have people say, "Gosh, you look so well, you look great. You look as if you've lost a lot of weight." The effect is more than physical. It encourages you to take hold of your life. You have a more youthful attitude about yourself and about what you can do, what you can still achieve. It also makes you far more fun to be with, and everyone enjoys your good looks.

You don't have to lose your femininity and sensuality as you mature. Some years ago, around 1961 I believe, I was flying to Paris to do a movie. The movie company had booked me on a Scandinavian jet that went over the pole and stopped off in Stockholm. While the plane was serviced, all the passengers were taken to a spa. The idea was to refresh us by letting us have a sauna.

It was an extraordinary experience. This motley group of women from the plane suddenly found themselves sitting around on slabs in the sauna, naked as newborns. I remember noticing a woman who I had seen sitting on the plane. She looked to be in her seventies, although she probably wasn't that old. You know how when you're younger you think anyone over fifty is seventy. I distinctly remember that she had the most beautiful figure, and lovely long hair. She had a shapely, rather Rubenesque type of body. I remember thinking, "How wonderful that one can look forward to having an alluring body at that age." I couldn't get over how graceful she was, like some artist's creation of ideal womanly beauty. It was a vision that remained in my mind. I decided I would try, as I got older, not to lose my sensuality.

Femininity and sexuality go hand in hand. It used to be thought that women lose interest in sex after menopause.

Down through the ages women have been stuck with the stigma that after passing childbearing age, they are suddenly of no interest to men. It's not true. But if you think it's true, then it will be true.

Anyone who has been married for a long time knows the importance of being responsive to the ways in which both individuals change. That certainly applies to our sexual lives as we grow older. Mature sex has to do with intimacy and trust and a deep closeness that develops over many years of understanding each other's needs. If you are openminded and positive, you can find a profound warmth that might not have the explosiveness of youth, but that has its own tremendous value. There must be a strong sense of consideration present in the bedroom, and if expectations are commensurate with reality, it is possible to still share moments that can express the feelings of love and respect that have developed over a lifetime.

I think it's important for a woman to try to maintain a certain sense of mystery about herself, and I think this can go on up to any age. I'm a real traditionalist in this realm, because I continue to believe that there's a certain quality in female sexuality that must be held back, not readily revealed. To keep that sense of feminine mystery, try to look at yourself as the man you're with would. Even if you've been together a long time, it isn't necessary to let him see you doing every little personal thing. Why should you struggle into your pantyhose in his view? Leave him wondering about why your eyelashes look so long and curly. It will make both of you feel more like you were courting, which for most people was a delightful time of anticipation and discovery. I know we are living in a more open and frank world than the one in which we grew up. But a little modesty always becomes a woman.

When it comes to our appearance, it's so easy to give up or

I believe that making the effort to take care of yourself in every way keeps you looking and feeling your best.

to get lazy. I feel it's worth it to continue to present yourself as a woman of loveliness and dignity, a woman who feels good and knows she's looking her best. You'll continue to attract attention as a feminine, sexual person. The right kind of attention never has to stop, unless you want it to.

7

Gazing Toward Tomorrow

AN EPILOGUE

In the late 1950s we moved to Malibu, where the magnificent sunsets that filled the winter sky every evening were events to be anticipated and savored. Peter and I sat in our living room one evening watching the changing panorama, as celestial shades of first pale rose, then apricot, and finally brilliant orange washed above the horizon. Streaks of high, thin clouds were transformed from white to deep turquoise to smoky navy as the daylight faded and the ocean disappeared into blackness. I turned to Peter and said, "I am totally happy at this moment. If my life ended three minutes from now, I would have felt that I had lived life to the fullest."

I was a young woman at the time, flush with contentment from my marriage, my children, my career. Perhaps I was moved by the exquisite drama of the sunset, but I hope I would always feel as I did that day, at any point in my life. I don't think any of us can honestly say we haven't succeeded in living as good a life as we could have under the circumstances. None of us should feel regret for the road not taken. There comes a point where we have to accept that we made the best choices in the past, and then we can feel confident we'll do the same in the days ahead.

I think we make an effort to live healthy lives because we all want to feel that we haven't let ourselves down. We all have a potential, as human beings. If we abuse ourselves, day in, day out, for months and years on end, we're not being fair to ourselves. So there comes a day of reckoning when we say, Am I going to continue this way, letting my body go, and be limited by lack of exercise, or am I going to pull my physical self together and feel as good as I can with what I've got? Feeling as good as we can with what we have, feeling that we haven't let ourselves down, is terribly important as we think about getting the most out of the future. It's never too late to change, you know.

I have friends who say they feel guilty if they spend time on themselves exercising. I feel the better you take care of yourself, the more you can bring to your relationships—with your husband, your children and grandchildren, all the people in your life. By being involved in life in a hopeful way, you reward yourself, and your enthusiasm is very compelling for others to be around.

I've been daydreaming a lot lately, envisioning a piece of land where I can create the kind of garden I'd like to have, where I'll enjoy the luxury of space and privacy. I already find myself putting things away that I'll move to my country house, even though it doesn't exist yet, except in my imagination. When I find this magical spot, it will open up whole new worlds for Peter and me.

There's a lot I haven't had the chance to do yet, in my life. I have so much to look forward to. And so do you.

*The publisher would like to express gratitude to the following people who
contributed their time, energy, and creativity:*

Jackie Aher
Linda Arnold
Robin Arzt
Delores Childers
Diane Gallagher
John Hunter
Judith Neuman-Cantor
Rita Sabatini
Susan Schwartz
Martha Schwerin
Rick Young

*If you would like more information about the "Angela Lansbury's Positive Moves"
videotape, call Wood Knapp Video, Los Angeles, CA, 1-800-331-6839.*